MW01016282

Redefining the Win
for Jr. High Small Groups

Redefining the Win
for Jr. High Small Groups

Published by Standard Publishing, Cincinnati, Ohio
www.standardpub.com

Copyright © 2010 by CHRIST IN YOUTH

Printed in: United States of America
Editors: Kelly Carr and Dana Wilkerson
Cover and interior design: Thinkpen Design, Inc., www.thinkpendesign.com

ISBN 978-0-7847-2320-3

16 15 14 13 12 11 10   1 2 3 4 5 6 7 8 9

A Rock Your Face Off
Jr. High Resource

Redefining the Win
for Jr. High Small Groups

Strategies, Tips, and Encouragement for Leaders and Volunteers

Johnny Scott

Standard
PUBLISHING

Cincinnati, Ohio

For the girl I met in jr. high, stalked in high school, and married in college, Jen.

To my dearest friends, the Christ In Youth family, thanks for allowing me to work on this book.

Thanks to the staff who works on the Jr. High Believe tour for all your listening and feedback.

I would also like to thank my youth pastors, Randy and Troy, for loving me as a jr. high kid.

Josh Finklea helped fan a flame in my heart for jr. high kids for which I will forever be indebted.

My thoughts in this book would not have been possible if not for the jr. high summit group that patiently teaches me what it means to truly love jr. high kids. I'll never forget the look on Marko's face over 6 years ago at a Believe event in Cincinnati at some of my comments about jr. high intentionality in ministry. I'm humbled at your investment in the Believe tour and long-suffering commitment to me as a jr. high leader.

Thanks in no particular order to the greatest group of jr. high leaders I have the pleasure of hanging with: Corrie Boyle, Kurt Brandemihl, Jeff Buell, April Diaz, Ken Elben, Heather Flies, Andy Jack, Mark Janzen, Kurt Johnston, Brooklyn Lindsey, Sean Meade, Alan Mercer, Mark Oestreicher, Jason Raitz, Alan Ramsey, Ken Rawson, Nate Rice, Christina Robertson, Phil Shinners, and Scott Rubin.

Thanks to Chase Allcott, Jayson French, Andy Hansen, Chris Jefferson, Patrick Snow, Eric Timm, Jordan Howerton, and Chad Monahan for constantly reminding me that a large part of me will always be a jr. high kid.

Thank you Dale Reeves for walking the road with me. I look forward to our cup of coffee in Cincy next time!

Riley, Aiden, and Finn: I can't wait to walk with you through your jr. high years; you are the 3 best buddies a dad could ever ask for.

Aside from my salvation in Jesus Christ, I am most thankful for the gift of Jennifer in my life. Her contribution to my ministry and work on this book can't be put into words.

Finally, Jen and I want to say thanks to all 6 of our awesome parents. It is not the divorce that will define my life, but how our God works in all things to bring glory to himself.

Contents

1: Jr. Highers Are People, Too 7

2: Your Real Goal 17

3: Rules Schmules 34

4: Great Expectations and How to Lower Them 49

5: Get Out of the Way! 57

6: Parents Are #1 66

7: Making Friends 82

8: Sometimes the Best Wins Are Not in Small Group . . . 95

9: Build a Fire and Dance Around It 103

10: You Can Do This . . . and You Should 114

Notes 128

About the Author 128

Foreword

When my friend Johnny Scott told me he was writing a book about jr. high small groups, I was thrilled. To my knowledge this book is the first of its kind, and it is much needed! In my experience as a jr. high youth pastor, there are few things, if any, more worth the time and effort than small groups.

For years, Johnny Scott has been the director of Believe, an incredible 2-day event designed specifically for jr. highers that tours the country every year; in fact, that's how the 2 of us met. The ministry I lead was considering creating a Believe-like event for our own jr. highers, and I decided to check out a Believe weekend to see what ideas I could borrow. (*Steal* would be a more truthful definition, but Christians don't *steal* from each other.)

The event was incredible . . . there were lights, cameras, and tons of action! It was one of the biggest, loudest, most exciting jr. high events I had ever seen. But here's the best part (why Johnny wrote this book and why I'm so excited about it): Johnny Scott's heart doesn't bleed for big, loud, crazy events like Believe—it bleeds for individual kids. Johnny is passionate about jr. high kids, and he recognizes the importance small groups play in their faith development. That's why every Believe weekend puts a huge emphasis on small groups, it's why Johnny leads a jr. high small group every week in his home church, and it's why he is the perfect person to write a book like *Redefining the Win for Jr. High Small Groups*. You might think Johnny would have written a book called, *Why Super, Big, Loud, Awesome Events in Crowded Arenas Full of Jr. High Kids Are the Wave of the Future*, because that would help Believe grow and would help pay his bills. But I'm so glad that he wrote *this* book.

Jr. high small groups are high-maintenance, messy, and frustrating. They seem to go wrong more often than they go right, and they seem to scare away more leaders than they attract. At least that's how they often feel in my youth group. But maybe that's only true because we're looking at them in the wrong light; perhaps it's time we redefine the win!

—Kurt Johnston,

jr. high pastor, Saddleback Church

1

Jr. Highers Are People, Too

It all starts here. I hope you think small groups are essential to mentoring jr. highers. Chances are, if you're reading this book, then you are already working with kids and genuinely care. I hope this book will convince, empower, and excite you about your jr. high small group! And while there is no magic blue pill to make your small group time 100 percent effective overnight, there are amazing strides that every small group can instantly take starting right now in this chapter. Let's dive in.

The philosophy for doing jr. high small groups starts with you and your perspective of who kids are in Christ, then it builds on some simple, but indispensable, tools you'll need. Jr. high small groups are so critical because not only do they meet kids' needs in the here and now, they also lay a framework for experiencing the church throughout life.

A Necessary Shift

If you want a rock your face off small group experience, then you have to start here—by realizing and treating your kids like they are real people, too. It may seem so simple—and obvious—but it is one of the largest obstacles in working with jr. highers, and it will yield maximum impact.

You are dedicating some precious time to what I feel may be the most kingdom-impacting investment you will ever make! Not only are you a great steward, you are also brave. The phrase *jr. higher* strikes fear into the hearts of many. There are many reasons for this. The jr. high years can be best summed up as crisis years. Kids are whisked from Matchbox® cars and Barbie® dolls to cliques, new complex social structures, and the stark realization that budding pubescent boys whose voices are changing apparently can't wear sweatpants to school anymore (due to certain physical realities).

Many volunteers are stoked about working with jr. highers because they had awful experiences during those years. The mere mention of the jr. high years often brings on a slew of emotional stories from adults. The most common advice given to young teens is to simply "make it through." This age group has become the punch line to jokes, and is used to explain anything extreme in nature or outside the margins for normal human behavior. No doubt this stereotype has been well deserved. The best place to start a small group—or improve one—is to realize that jr. highers are people, too.

If the church janitorial staff and others had their way, we would lock these kids in padded rooms the entire time that they are at church. When you say, "jr. high ministry," most people think of big games and herding cats. But you know differently. Jr. highers are in the thick of deciding how important faith will be in their lives. By the time they get to high school, many of them have already formulated the foundational parts of their belief structure. What are your perceptions of jr. high kids? They often make us laugh because of their sharp wit—many times on accident. The goofier we act the more they seem to identify with us. We have to look past the zits, awkward moments, and what might be perceived as failed small group sessions to see that these teens are testing, feverishly growing, changing, processing, and even hurting. As in all things, God begins to work in us first, shaping and molding us in turn to shape and mold others. Ask yourself if you are ready to change *first*. This is where a true understanding of what you have been called to do must begin.

Speak into Their Lives

Your influence in the lives of kids can be greater and bear more fruit with just a little bit of wisdom and tweaking. Just like you, jr. high teens can hear, understand, rethink, and be reasoned with.

So You Get Paid

As you read through this chapter, here are some additional questions for you to ponder:

* How are you modeling small group ministry?
* Are you setting your small group leaders up for success?
* Are any of your small group volunteers easily intimidated? Communicate with them in a confident and clear way. Give them concrete examples of how small groups can and should operate in your ministry.
* What can you learn after every small group experience? Gain more confidence by asking yourself what you took away from the experience; then decipher the results.
* How can you use this same perspective to encourage your volunteers?
* What is the morale of your volunteer leaders concerning the effectiveness of your small groups?

Simply stated, jr. highers can change. Unfortunately, far too many youth workers give up on the simplest truths and start looking for trends, fads, and newfangled ways to communicate with kids. Perhaps the time-tested methods for relating to young teens work best. We have to speak consistently into their lives. Have you abandoned your right to speak into the lives of kids by accepting the lie that they don't listen or don't care, or that there is some impenetrable layer of mistrust that has slowly developed between their world and yours?

It may be true that there is a barrier of mistrust, but the key to overcoming this hurdle is to embrace the sacred tradition of speaking into the lives of teens. We must speak courage, hope, faith, God's Word, laughter, discipline, and character into the lives of those whom God calls us to mentor. When you say you want to be a jr. high small group leader, you are joining a band of people who agree to raise the social consciousness concerning the value of our most precious possession—our kids! You are acting out God's command, "Direct your children onto the right path, and when they are older, they will not leave it" (Proverbs 22:6).

When you start to realize that jr. high kids are people, others will join hands with you and invest in them, too. Some will come alongside and actually get dirty with you. Others may just look at you from the outside and pity you. They may applaud your efforts and even throw a few bucks your way. When you make the shift that kids are actually people and you believe that you can speak into their lives, then you are on the way to a fruitful experience. Small shifts in your thinking pave the way for many other things. You believe that jr. high kids are capable of amazing feats. This is a much different philosophy than simply providing entertainment to occupy their time in hopes that they "make it through." In his book *Soul Searching*, sociologist Christian Smith presents data from case studies in which kids were followed over a period of 4 years. They were asked numerous questions about faith and church. Christian comments that the overarching message our society—both the church and the non-churched—has communicated to kids is "have fun, don't mess up."[1]

How has this attitude permeated our ministry methods? I've noticed a doom and gloom outlook on the effect of youth ministry on high schoolers as they leave to go to college. Many high school kids are naively optimistic. They have felt "prepared" since they got their driver's license—but are they prepared to launch out into the real world? In surveying the virtual report card on youth ministry, some leaders have shifted blame, and others have tried to change methods to

So You're a Volunteer

Please know that as a volunteer you fill the most important role! You are exemplifying a servant spirit to the whole body of believers by choosing to mentor jr. high teens—one of the most significant ministries in the church. Somebody, somewhere, saw something in you that perhaps you didn't even see yourself! It could have been the ability to really be authentic with kids. Perhaps other leaders liked you and wanted to serve with you in this area of the church. God has designed more for kids in these crucial years than just "making it through."

You are a priest, you know! You are part of the new royal priesthood (1 Peter 2:9). God makes no distinction in the New Testament between professional Christians and lay workers. Be affirmed that your ministry is strategic for the kingdom of God. Do something to keep learning how to be a better, wiser youth worker. God will bless your diligence.

get a different outcome. Many fingers have been pointed at North American youth ministry as a failure. And our inability to effectively reach teens will begin in the jr. high years if we don't purpose to do more than call them to "have fun, don't mess up." The college years directly mirror the crisis years of jr. high. I believe that if we can set up good patterns in jr. high ministry, then we can change the pattern of kids going off to college.

Jr. highers respond to adults who want to help them and who view them as people God is transforming into new creations. And really powerful things happen when the adult community communicates to a teen, "You are a valued member of our society."

Why It Matters

You may be asking questions like these:

✦ Why should I allow small groups to soak up so much of the valuable time I have with kids every week?
✦ Why does our church place such an emphasis on small groups?

Just how important is a small group ministry at the jr. high level? We have no widely-accepted structure for walking with kids from childhood to adulthood aside from the popcorn approach of Sunday school lessons, faith events, and family outings. What methods do we point to that monitor how an individual kid is processing the crisis of jr. high? We are helping kids navigate the pathway to adulthood. They want to go there but they have lots of lessons to learn along the way—and it is going to take a lot of patience . . . and a long time. Many of them are afraid to go there. They don't understand the new world they are trying to reach.

Every kid is unique. Kids like different songs and TV shows for different reasons. They have different home stories—but they *all* love to have their names remembered! And they all need a faith of their own that will hold them together during life's crises (a.k.a. jr. high).

As youth ministry in America is just finishing its 4th decade, a lot of criticism has come due to the numbers showing churched kids falling away from church attendance and major faith commitments during their early college years. Consider these parallels between the jr. high years and college years:

The Jr. High Years

* an abrupt introduction to change

1. physical (puberty)

2. social (more complex relationships)

3. mental (new education routines, higher expectations)

* a need for time and space to process new environments, feelings, and changes

The College Years

* a heightened sense of change and independence

1. physical (not as drastic as puberty, but upheaval can result in physical changes)

2. social (high school methods for interpreting relationships and making choices have been removed)

3. mental (new schedule, more freedom, the highest expectations yet)

* a need for time and space to process new environments, feelings, and changes

Because of the striking parallels between these 2 critical junctures in life, it is absolutely crucial that we lay a solid foundation of good habits in jr. high kids to fall back on for the second eruption of social change coming their way during the college years. We need to create a culture in jr. high small groups in which it is instinctive for kids to run to healthy relationships within the church during moments of crisis. Additionally, we should be creating an environment in which they feel permission to doubt, question, and wrestle with difficult faith questions. In a nutshell, we are showing them that every realm of their lives is spiritual. The walls that block God out are being torn down so that they can live a life where faith is not compartmentalized. (By the way, their parents may be struggling with this very thing.) This will arm teens with the ability to handle the next transition in life in which they will physically leave their parents, but hopefully not abandon them emotionally.

This correlation of feelings and issues that connect college and jr. high kids together can be a perfect pairing for ministry. They really do understand each other on a deep level. Many college kids sense the need for a new and greater connection to the larger church, and jr. high ministry is a great place to let them serve.

Love Kids and the Church

It is not the intent of a jr. high small group to calm all crises that jr. high kids experience. The greater goal is to introduce them to the larger framework of the kingdom of God—the adventure, the stakes, the history, the anticipation, and the sweet community. In the midst of this growth process, a kid will learn to deal with the difficulties of jr. high within the protective community of the church. The small group structure should not be an end in itself, but a portal to the larger church community. This happens largely through the language and perspective offered by the small group leader. And if real growth happens successfully during the jr. high years, the natural response of a college freshman in the midst of a changing environment will be to seek out the nurturing and community found in the framework of the church. It helped him once, why not again?

For that reason, to be an effective small group leader for jr. high kids you need to have a genuine love not only for kids, but also for the church. It would be counterproductive for a teen to desire to return to the safety of a specific group *only,* and not possess a view that all the good things about his small group experience were true because of God's overall design of his one church. It is here at the jr. high level—the first potentially catastrophic life phase—that a kid should be introduced to the larger ministry of the church. The gateway to that introduction is through small peer groups with adult guides who are proactively equipping them with the tools to make it through the next cataclysmic life change—college. It starts here, and I hope that gets you really stoked about jr. high ministry!

Not too long ago I had a phone interview for an article that would appear in a Christian magazine. One of the questions the writer submitted prior to the interview was this: "Why do tweens and jr. high kids need their

So You're in a Small Church

Did you know that the typical Protestant church in America has an average worship attendance of 89 adults? Sixty percent of people who attend church in North America on Sunday do so in a congregation with 100 or fewer adults in worship.[2] If you are doing jr. high ministry in a small church, you have some built-in bonuses and a few hurdles, too. One great thing is that your small group already has a dynamic that many large jr. high ministries are striving for! You most likely know the stories of every kid in your small group because you personally know their parents and siblings. This is so valuable in working with kids. You do not have to fight against many of the silos that exist in larger churches. And as we talked about in this chapter, presenting kids with a larger framework of the church outside of jr. high ministry is much more tangible for kids to grasp in a small church. Be encouraged!

own music, when they can just listen to the music now that they will eventually listen to when they are older teens?" I steered the interview to the theme of what is currently wrong with our approaches to walking beside the youth in the church as they grow up. We have too often settled for raising children with a "just get through it" mentality. Some adults expect jr. high kids to rush through these years and get to high school. Jr. high kids are at a different stage developmentally, so they need their own music. We must believe to the core that jr. highers are people, too. ✦

Do This Now

1. Remember your own jr. high experience. Who impacted you most, and how did they do it? Write them a note of gratitude.

2. Choose a kid in your group and attend a function of his or hers outside of small group. Communicate to this teen that you came because you care about everything in his or her life. Then evaluate how taking that step made an impact on the development of the teen's identity in your small group time.

3. Picture one of your jr. highers in high school, then in college, getting married, and finally, with children of his own. Examine how you look at your teens. How does this affect what you expect from them, and how you unintentionally treat them?

2

Your Real Goal

Have you ever returned home from a youth ministries conference with great enthusiasm about your new small group master plan? You have the best volunteers ever (or you *are* the best volunteer ever), and you've communicated to the parents and church staff in meticulous detail about how the program will be a success. The curriculum was field-tested by the other leaders and chosen by the jr. high leadership team. But somewhere between the back-to-school kickoff and Christmas break the impact you envisioned fizzled out.

What went wrong? It just didn't seem to add up.

Let me propose a step backward. What was the defined win for small groups? What was the real goal, and how did you evaluate it? How did you celebrate that win and then communicate it to the kids who were with you in the circle?

What's Your Point of View?

I'd like to suggest a new way of looking for growth in teens—focusing on events that happen all the time, yet often go uncelebrated or even unnoticed. This is a new take on defining the win for what happens in your small group time.

Point of view can be everything. I was taught this lesson early on. I can still hear all of my grandmother's quips and songs, and I can see the quaint pillow stitchings that promoted having a good attitude. She

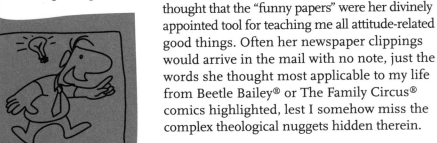

thought that the "funny papers" were her divinely appointed tool for teaching me all attitude-related good things. Often her newspaper clippings would arrive in the mail with no note, just the words she thought most applicable to my life from Beetle Bailey® or The Family Circus® comics highlighted, lest I somehow miss the complex theological nuggets hidden therein.

Perspective lessons like these come flooding back every time God needs to remind me that my view is somehow skewed. Many of us who work with jr. highers need a refreshing perspective shift to free our minds of unrealistic expectations and focus our attention on the uncelebrated, unnoticed growth happening in kids. This process is called *defining the win*. What is the real goal? Everyone involved in your jr. high ministry needs to know what it is.

Not the Happiest Place on Earth

Before we redefine the win and look at our real goal, let's remember why we got into mentoring jr. highers in the first place. You may have decided in your own adolescence that you wanted to work with kids. Perhaps you wanted to give back because relevant jr. high ministry touched you, and you wanted to follow some amazing youth worker who modeled Christ for you. You remember how tough the pubescent years were for you and feel like you can relate to and help kids. Maybe someone who saw potential in you persuaded you to join the ranks of youth workers in your church. (Don't be bitter—many others have been tricked into it as well.)

From among these good intentions a damaging ideal can arise to destroy our joy. This beast has devoured too many would-be great jr. high workers. I pray that you can be saved from the youth-coach-killing disease known as "Small Group Fantasy Land." (Out of respect for those who have fallen before, please read *Small Group Fantasy Land* with a scary voice.)

Small Group Fantasy Land (SGFL) starts with a preconceived notion and expectation that somehow our amazing spiritual insights will fall on unsuspecting victims, rendering them helpless, awash in our awe-inspiring wisdom. In short, young Billy is never going to look at you and say, "Your lesson tonight has touched my life in a profound way. Because of your sacrifice in sharing this insight with us I am compelled to implement this spiritual discipline in all facets of my daily walk with Christ." *It's simply not going to happen!* So why do we beat ourselves up when that pipe dream doesn't materialize? In the meantime there are all kinds of incredible spiritual things happening (or just on the verge) every week at our small groups that we brush over. By reevaluating the real goals, we won't stifle some of the steps for which our kids need encouragement now.

Working with jr. highers can be an emotional roller-coaster ride. Bottled up in these dynamically developing people we find explosive ingredients ready to ignite at any moment. Just when you think you know what kids are thinking, they completely surprise you. If you've been investing in jr. highers' lives very long, no doubt you already have some great stories centered around awkward moments when someone blurted something out. The fact is, you never know what they are thinking or—even more frightening—if they will *say* what

So You Get Paid

It's easier to keep a great jr. high volunteer than find and train new ones. Be honest, keep your word, encourage, give time off without guilt, and communicate consistently.

The best method I've ever seen used to get new volunteers is to identify someone you think is gifted, ask him or her to lunch and present the idea, and offer time to pray about it. Many people don't serve because they have never been plainly asked.

Defining and communicating the win to your volunteer leaders and teens is key. With the right expectations and goals being communicated, jr. high small groups can cultivate an environment for positive experiences. This isn't about lowering the bar for leaders' expectations; it's about everyone on board understanding the goals for ministry in early adolescent small groups.

* How have you communicated your goals in the past effectively?
* What attempts to do so have been ineffective?
* What practical steps can you take from this chapter to communicate your goals more effectively?

they're thinking. These moments bring joy and laughter and remind us that we love working with jr. high kids.

Jr. High Kids Rock

Robert was a normal 14-year-old boy in many aspects except 1. He was preparing to tour the country with me, singing in front of thousands of kids. Realizing that this would be a critically formative experience for Robert, I wanted the chance to speak into his life. I jumped into classic youth pastor mode and summarized this mountaintop chapter in life he was about to enter. I talked about the opportunity to minister to his peers and grow spiritually himself. I felt like Bob Ross painting a masterpiece that would certainly result in a spectacular youth ministry moment. I could see the beautiful Thomas Kinkade painting depicting that turning point discussion. As the last inspiring word left my mouth, I checked for the look of illumination on Robert's face. With all my good intentions in hand, I truly expected to see his worldview change right before my eyes. Robert answered with the sincerity that only true innocence could convey, "Yeah, man, I think I am going to grow tall enough this spring to be able to dunk!"

I couldn't help but laugh out loud. Not at Robert, but at myself. Had I forgotten that the real lessons are in the relationships? From time to time we need to be reminded of just how much fun it is to work with jr. high kids. Investing in kids isn't rocket science. It's about relationship.

What you are doing in building relationships with kids is significant. Check this out. A dedicated lifelong jr. high worker, Heather, knows how to look for the win. The first time Lydia's mom tried to introduce Lydia to Heather in church, Lydia saw Heather from 20 feet away, turned, and ran the other direction! Still, week in and week out, Heather made a point to approach and make a connection with Lydia. Lydia almost seemed put off by Heather's attempt to reach out to her.

Heather heard Lydia talk about being on the color guard team (a mix between flag corps and cheerleading) and told Lydia she wanted to attend a competition. The only competition that would work in Heather's schedule was 32 miles away on a night that would have been Heather's only night at home in quite some time. Heather decided to make the trip, hoping that the effort would help in building a relational >>

Defining the Win Challenge

Some people suffer from a condition far different than SGFL, but it, too, can destroy the health and spiritual growth in a small group. If you feel like you have little to offer jr. high kids, I hope this chapter changes your outlook on jr. high small groups. Perhaps you feel as though you were placed in a position of ministry where you're not effective and skilled . . . and your frustration is growing. Maybe you feel like you've been reading lessons to bored kids instead of investing in their spiritual lives, or you have been spending 25 minutes trying to get 6th grade girls to be quiet. Don't despair! This is for you.

God's Word says that he alone hands out all authority (Psalm 24:1, 2). You may not always understand how God is using you to touch kids' lives, but I believe that his word is powerful and will produce a fruit because he promised it to us. Take comfort in Isaiah 55:8-11:

"My thoughts are nothing like your thoughts," says the LORD. "And my ways are far beyond anything you could imagine. For just as the heavens are higher than the earth, so my ways are higher than your ways and my thoughts higher than your thoughts. The rain and snow come down from the heavens and stay on the ground to water the earth. They cause the grain to grow, producing seed for the farmer and bread for the hungry. It is the same with my word. I send it out, and it always produces fruit. It will accomplish all I want it to, and it will prosper everywhere I send it."

If you have been placed in a position of authority with a small group, know that God will be faithful to fulfill his Word, and he will give you the gifts needed for your group. One strength of the body of Christ is that we have different skill sets. Some have the ability to teach, some are funny, some are athletic, and others are great listeners and counselors. You may possess a number of abilities that would attract jr. high kids. If you are struggling with whether or not working with jr. highers is your calling, then I challenge you to prayerfully think over these insights:

✦ Who influenced you in your formative years, and what Bible stories do you remember the most because of their teaching? No doubt those important people taught you Bible stories, but perhaps what you remember the most is how they listened, loved, and took time to invite you to simply live life with them. That is what kept you coming to hear them share lessons from God's Word.

>> bridge. She attended the competition and was at the corner of the floor, camera posed, cheering her heart out for the 4½-minute routine!

As she was greeting kids the next week at church, Heather came upon Lydia. It was as if Heather had been her BFF for years, as Lydia greeted her with the kind of squeals puppies and jr. high girls have in common. Heather was blown away to even get a second look—but acted as if she'd been best buds with Lydia for years.

The payoff would have never come if Heather hadn't been consistent even in the face of apathy week after week. She had chosen to define the win as getting the chance to just say hello to Lydia whenever she could. Then she seized the opportunity to make an impact when it presented itself.

- Do you want to do something with your life investment that makes the most impact possible? The greatest work we can do is found in Psalm 78:4: "Tell the next generation the praiseworthy deeds of the Lord, his power, and the wonders he has done" (*NIV*).
- Are you trusting God—through your obedience—that he will work in ways you don't understand? God doesn't always let us see the transformation before our eyes just because we want to. More times than not we have to do our part by investing in kids, trusting that God will water and feed those seeds.

My prayer is that by rethinking what constitutes wins for the small group experience, God is showing you what unique gifts you bring to the table. This shift in thinking can begin to unleash the youth leader God intends for you to be. Keep reading! You can do this.

Trust God and Listen More

Give yourself a break. It's not all on you. Years from now, God's Word will continue to shape and feed the teens entrusted to you today. As you trust that the Holy Spirit is doing his work, you just need to be obedient.

Jesus pointed out in the parable of the soils (Matthew 13) that not all soil is ready to receive the seed. Some soil is rocky, some is thorny, and some is compacted like the road. Jr. high kids have a type of soil, too. Only God can change soil. Don't feel like your lesson has to till the ground, plant the seed, water, feed, and raise the sun every week. Some weeks are just OK so that we will be able to tell them apart from the really awesome ones.

A 20-year veteran jr. high worker named Alan says, "Be ready. Because the lesson is not always the lesson!" Things creep up that can be wonderful and life changing. Sometimes we get tunnel vision with things like laying out every nuance of how we think the world will end, while kids may be more busy processing how you talked to your spouse on the phone before small group began.

Many jr. highers feel like life is "happening to them." They have a sense of being out of control. Although the discussion time will be awkward and the lesson's points may never be communicated as well as you know they could, relinquish control. Letting kids continually take the reins will slowly reassure them that small group is a place where they can safely practice processing faith issues out loud. And it will be one place where they can feel that life is *not* happening *to* them.

Another jr. higher's authentic comment on the lesson (even if presented poorly) is better than your best-practiced answer. One major complaint from kids is that they often feel misunderstood. There is so much peace and freedom found in feeling understood. There is not much else more agitating than *not* feeling understood. I felt this frustration in Greg. I remember talking with him over a few months about his life, future, and father. I kept giving Greg advice by telling him stories from my own life—and none of my words seemed to bring him any clarity or comfort. I saw the angst welling up in him as we continued our discussion. He actually looked like the frustration was so welled up in his gut that it was about to explode. He couldn't quite put it into words. He couldn't phrase it in a way that made him feel like he resonated with me at an emotional level where I could truly emphasize with him. Greg wanted me to be able to walk the road with him.

In all my attempts to bring wisdom, guidance, assurance, and perspective, I failed because they all involved me talking. I have talked with tons of jr. highers all over the country and have failed many times at listening my way into ministering to them. Greg's release moment was when I finally ran out of comebacks and simply had to listen. It was then that he felt assurance and God's love touching him through me.

Jr. highers hear more than we give them credit for. Celebrating healthy involvement on any level is crucial! Practice trying to understand. This starts with listening more.

My wife and I love our home church and are very involved in its ministry. Wednesday nights are the best night of the week for me to be consistent in my presence there. This is the night we offer deeper Bible study for our teens. This semester our jr. high pastor, Matt, and I have been struggling with how much impact we are having in the kids' lives.

We really want to meet them where they are at with the Bible, so we asked them to submit questions they'd like answered. Here is the list of some of the questions they turned in (excluding the extra ones about animals and Heaven—that is a serious concern in the lives of middle school teens!):

1. Where did sin come from?
2. What boundaries should we set when in a dating relationship?
3. How far is too far (in a dating relationship)?
4. Do animals go to Heaven?
5. How do I convince my friend to come to church?
6. Is it OK to look at your wife with lust after you're married?
7. If God has all power, why doesn't he just kill Satan and bring world peace?
8. Does the Bible say that you'd go to Hell if you committed suicide?
9. What was it like when Jesus went to Heaven?
10. People say that drinking is a sin, but Jesus himself drank wine—so what's the deal?
11. How can I get more involved with God?
12. If God created all things, where did sin come from?

13. What is Heaven like?
14. Does God put people in ranks in Heaven (if someone loves God with all their heart vs. loving with only a little of their heart)?
15. Was Jesus really born on Christmas? If not, why is it called Christmas? And where did Jesus go when he died because he had all of our sins?
16. Is it true that ghosts and spirits are things that do not go to Hell?
17. How old do you think people should be to have a boyfriend or girlfriend?
18. Does God love gay people too?
19. What are the signs that Jesus is coming back?
20. If God loves everyone, why do people go to Hell?
21. Where was God before he died?
21. How can I resist temptation?
23. Why don't we talk about the Old Testament a lot in the church?
24. When you die, do you go to Heaven or do you stay dead until Jesus comes back?
25. If God didn't want us to have dirty thoughts, why does he let them happen?

Jr. high kids are very spiritual. They think about spiritual things, and they live and operate in very spiritual ways. It is amazing what listening can do to infuse a ministry with new life and excitement. We were banging our heads against a wall a few weeks ago looking for real connection with teens. This list has just hit me upside the head! We now have more gripping topics that we have to look into God's Word to solve than we can accomplish in a whole semester! Go figure.

Time to Define Some Wins

Jr. highers are often not capable of communicating and processing the point of small group sessions in ways that will meet the SGFL standards. This is a developmental issue. Many leaders get frustrated

One great thing about a small church is that it is family. You can be relaxed and take a laid-back approach because of the familiarity with your kids and their families. Ministry is deeper and more holistic when you have the knowledge and foundation of where a kid is coming from.

But when you want to deviate from the laid-back approach and make a significant impression, a little extra effort in planning your events can go a long way in communicating to your teens that their events are special. They will notice when you go above and beyond. Ask the whole church to join in a ceremony inviting kids into middle school ministry, dress up and serve them a special meal, then have adults say a few affirming things about each kid or give words of advice for this new chapter in life. It will yield great benefits in the lives of your kids.

that kids don't seem to *get* the spiritual points being communicated. The truth is that many times they conceptually understand the themes we are delivering—they are simply wrestling with communicating their thoughts.

We all want to see life change in teens. Many jr. high youth ministries have discovered the importance of assimilating caring adults into the program who value doing life with adolescents. These ministries have also adopted some form of small group meeting time as a part of their larger vision for ministering to jr. highers. Almost everyone agrees that this small group interaction time can be effective. But after being inundated with the vast amount of curriculum and tools for small group leaders, have you ever found yourself back to square one, asking the question of what to do with jr. high small groups?

The answer is in defining what a great small group meeting looks like. In other words, identify the goal and communicate it to the teens in a way that resonates with them.

Without a new way of defining and communicating the wins during every small group session, many leaders feel like they've failed. Teens get frustrated just like we do, and they pick up on our disappointment with small group time. Some leaders have unrealistic expectations of jr. highers. But the fact is that many teens are not capable of articulating what God is doing in their hearts and minds. Many of these small group experiences are seeds that may not be seen for years. We want adolescents to have that breakthrough.

The act of processing faith issues in an environment with caring adults is a pathway we want to familiarize teens with. This in itself is a major win for a small group. Jr. highers are like wet cement. Very quickly they will be set in their ways. How awesome it is when teens begin to process their thoughts about faith and life in the context of a church small group! That's the payoff, and it can happen.

Constantly redefine the win! Question what you do now, and don't be afraid to experiment with redefining your jr. high small group wins. Here are some win-defining ideas from what others are doing:

- Define the win as 1 kid finally accepting the hug you have been offering for months.
- Define the win as kids not wanting to leave as soon as the official time is over.
- Define the win as someone remembering *anything* from last week.
- Define the win as pairing caring adults with teens.
- Define the win as trusting the Holy Spirit that more is getting through than meets the eye.
- Define the win as jr. highers simply coming back for more.
- Define the win as knowing adolescents feel loved and not manipulated.
- Define the win as adults being determined to look teens in the eye and simply listen as long as they need to talk. (If you did this at small group, it was a huge win!)
- Define the win as anything that shows you are building a relational bridge with a jr. higher!

Has a kid told you about an event happening in his life this week? It wasn't just conversation. Read between the lines. Are your teens anxious, do they want you to attend their events but don't know how to ask?

Unless they are being forced to attend small group by their parents, jr. highers do have other options. If they decided to come on their own to small group, that's a win.

Did a parent help bring them? That is a win because they feel strongly enough about their involvement to invest the time, gas, and hassle of dropping their teens off and picking them up. That is a huge win you needn't overlook. Did you get the chance to connect with that parent and say thanks? That is a bridge.

Did you get to appropriately touch every kid and say something below the surface level about who they are in God's eyes? If that is *all* you did, the whole evening was a hit! That doesn't happen at school and maybe not even at home.

Did someone bring a friend? That is a big deal if they trust you enough to let you in on their world with their friends.

Did someone express any thought that occurred to them during the week concerning last week's content? That is a huge win, and you must celebrate it. Encourage and praise any teen's attempt to take their faith into other parts of their lives.

Celebrate Wins Often

Follow-up is critical to successfully shifting into a new perspective of how you define your wins. There is danger in looking just once at what the wins are. We have to keep looking at what constitutes a win in our small group, or we run the risk of not getting to celebrate that win corporately. By omission it gets communicated that bringing a friend isn't important, that being honest about our feelings didn't matter, or that just coming back wasn't good enough tonight to meet the leader's approval. When we celebrate each win we are communicating to everyone involved that this is the real goal.

A common mistake youth workers make is expecting early adolescents to be able to communicate complex situations and feelings with adult terminology. Just because they can't clearly sum up the issues they are facing does not mean they aren't wrestling with them in real ways. This gap in their communication development leads workers to make assumptions that just aren't true. There are some things you can do to prevent falling into this pitfall that will stall the relationship-building journey with your jr. highers.

- Don't set the bar too low for them.
- Be prepared to listen closely to the heart of what they are trying to say.
- Introduce complex situations and questions, but be prepared to journey with them the whole way.
- Read between the lines, ask probing questions, and then sum up what you think they are saying.
- After you have communicated your summary, ask if you have understood them correctly.

We need to remember that kids have 1 foot in 2 separate worlds. Physically they look old enough to juggle adult situations and we find ourselves expecting that from them. But mentally jr. highers are wading through so much new information and brand new experiences that they can't process it all. This explains why they can operate at a highly cognitive level in one instance and then look at us like they are clueless just 10 minutes later.

Small group sharing is so important at this age. When kids hear one another stumble through an explanation of any emotion, it helps them learn to express for themselves. As an adult you may have an incredible story that nails the issue at hand, but there is a bigger success found when a group of kids stumble through discussing the faith process with each other in their own words.

Sometimes the greatest good you can do is to be there consistently. Your presence is far more important than any amazing illustration you can come up with to "change their lives." Life change is found in the ebb and flow of relationship, and it needs to be celebrated often.

Jr. High Kids Rock

Jr. high kids love craft time. We just are not allowed to call it that. Finding things to engage them on a tactile level is key. One such project during worship reminded me why we love working with jr. highers.

Some time ago we desired to engage kids in a more inter-active and responsive manner during our gathering times. We decided to invite them to write out their prayers on some long pieces of paper we had attached to a section of the wall. Kids were to go and write whatever they wanted during a slow song set. A few weeks later I was talking with some teens near this writing project and began to read over the entries of prayer and art on the wall. I started with one written in sparkly purple. The handwriting was neat and in bubbly-shaped letters. I was confident that it was a girl's prayer. I thought, *Is that a special class that only girls have in grade school, "How to write bubbly letters"? I don't have that font.*

· After reading a few more prayers, I ran across one that reinforced how much God loves jr. high workers who are willing to invest their time with kids. It embodied all the catastrophic emotion and turbulent change churning in the soul of a middle school kid. It read simply, "Help me in school—Sam."

Jr. high kids are great. Jesus loves them and hears them, and I was reminded about how awesome it is to work with them. God is looking for people (not just experts or theologians) to walk beside kids—willing adults who will just listen. I think you can do that. ✦

Do This Now

1. Celebrate some things today that often go unnoticed. Learn to listen between the lines. Many kids give us hints at what we should be celebrating without coming out and telling us. They may be joking about something that really is serious to them. Their outward emotions do not always reflect their true inward feelings. Listen, and help coach them.

2. Be consistent, even when it feels like you are getting nowhere relationally with someone. You never know which teen is on the brink of something great or something devastating.

3. Celebrate with other leaders. If a recent small group meeting was rough and kids didn't seem to pay attention, but leaders made an effort to listen to each kid, then acknowledge each other. Did someone attend a kid's event and make a point of contact outside small group time? That's a big win. Celebrate it!

4. Thank God for every victory! Did a quiet kid finally share out loud? Sometimes we get to see big steps in kids' lives, and other times we have to trust that God's pursuit (and our consistency) will make an impact.

Rules Schmules

Some people work with jr. high small groups for those brilliant moments that can only be explained by knowing there is a God who is big and is pursuing us all relentlessly. I like to call those times "Brittney moments."

Brittney had only been in church 3 times before. At 14 years old she had lots of questions and was eager to learn and grow. Then it happened. During a small group experience Brittney blurted out an answer that was so profoundly truthful, insightful, and introspectively honest that the entire group—adults included—were shell-shocked: "Why do I spend all this time worrying about what I look like and what other people think when the creator of the universe already formed me the way he wants me and loves me this way?" What a statement from the heart and mind of a teen! If she could come to terms with that truth now, how much more incredible is her faith journey going to be? Brittney's statement led to other great conversations with the other teens.

We get kids into small groups because great things can happen to propel them forward in their faith. Just one experience like this can keep leaders charged for months or even years. Unfortunately, we've all felt like we were on the brink of such a great moment when 1 of our 6th grade boys completely destroyed the momentum with a comment that disrupted the whole group. Yes, it is a strong possibility that he is the one who will most likely be a youth worker, too! But that does no good in the present when the group time has been destroyed—or so we feel. So we tell ourselves to trust that these eye-opening experiences are happening, and the seeds are being planted all the time—even when we don't always get the home-run experience of a "Brittney moment."

So what do you do when your group seems light-years away from such a breakthrough? While there isn't a magic formula for transforming your small group into a beacon for all spiritual truth, there are some things you can do now that will steer you in the right direction.

Setting the Tone

First of all, begin by creating a positive structured environment. Clear communication and some healthy ground rules can actually be fun. God has clearly communicated boundaries for our protection and continued growth. We find security and love in knowing our boundaries. Kids push back for the same reasons adults push on God . . . but they will respond to clear boundaries. Expect them to push back because that is part of the development process in jr. high.

Our desire is to get the kids on the small group boat and keep them on so that we can travel somewhere together that we can't go to by ourselves. We need those kids that give us fits because they are part of the crew. Meanwhile, the "good kids" attentively watch with perfect memory every nuance in our demeanor as we handle disruptive kids.

Here are some practical tips for establishing and maintaining some semblance of authority in your small group:

- Split up boys and girls. Sometimes it is completely necessary, not only because of a specific topic, but to have more control.
- Have adult leaders intentionally sit in the group.
- Pray with other leaders before kids arrive.
- Only make rules you plan on enforcing. You can't complain about what you permit.
- Try to see what lies behind the disruptive behavior. The presenting problem is rarely the real problem. For instance, what is going on in the teen's home or school life?
- You *have* to genuinely love them. The truth of this will seep out; they will know. Some of your kids have been wounded by adults in

the past. You will have to earn their respect. They won't respect you simply because you are nice.

* Know when to address an issue at a deeper level by getting others to help you. Not every problem should be worked out in the small group arena. Don't let a situation with 1 kid who has deeper issues ruin the whole group experience.

* Don't duck issues that you know you should confront. If you do, they will come back to haunt you! An old Native American proverb is worth your attention: "Listen to the whispers and you will never have to hear the screams."

Switching It Up

We need to remember that jr. high kids like and need structure. So much is changing in their worlds that they thrive and relax in an environment where they can depend on an order of things. They can get unexplainably tense when the smallest things change. You might think it odd that Suzie is crying because the group is eating s'mores inside instead of eating ice cream on the deck, due to the rain. By itself, that's not a big deal, but she might really be crying because that was the 10th thing that abruptly changed without her foreknowledge that day.

A friend of mine surprised his 7th grade daughter with expensive concert tickets to a show that everybody was dying to see. The suddenness of the surprise on the evening of the concert was more than the girl could handle. She didn't have several weeks to decide what to wear, and she hadn't gotten to brag at school or text for days about the anticipated event. There was no time to process the great gift. She ran to her room and cried all night, and the tickets were wasted!

Generally speaking, girls react differently than boys do, but it can kill a boy's spirit if he is excited to show that he finally remembered his Bible for the FIRST TIME EVER and the leader flippantly disregards the win because that night's agenda was a surprise service project!

Jr. high kids still need a bit of structure. However, there is something to be said about getting crazy and changing things a bit to spice up church on a rainy Wednesday night. Here are some practical tips for organizing your small group time:

* Warn kids about special nights in advance whenever you can. If you want to keep it a surprise, then tell them exactly that. "Next week is a surprise night; be ready for something different than our normal meeting time."
* Tell the kids how much hang-out time they have, and reward them after the teaching time with more leisure time if it's appropriate.
* Remember that kids are BUSY! Lots of things vie for their attention, so you need to work hard at mixing it up. For example, every now and then give them 15 minutes of quiet time to read the Bible passage so they can have the knowledge to engage in discussion time.
* As you try to strike a balance between structure and spontaneity, encourage moments of silence for thinking. After you throw out a question, let kids sit for a minute or 2 and think. In their structured lives, they don't get much time to do that.

Snacks Are Spiritual

Life happens around food. Many of Jesus' stories took place while heading somewhere to eat or leaving someplace where he and his disciples had just eaten. We all need food to sustain life. When we eat with someone and share in the community, something happens on a spiritual level. People talk more openly when they are eating. Most meetings just go better with food present; we let our guard down without even knowing it.

Don't let small group time be over when it is time for snacks. Keep on the lookout for meaningful conversations or breakthroughs in relationship building. This is a great time to dig in more with kids about something they might have alluded to earlier. The snack time allows a safe environment for you to have some more personal face time with kids on an individual level, with other kids and adult leaders present.

And don't skimp on the snacks! Kids are people too, so they know when snack time isn't important. (Read: NO FAKE OREO® COOKIES!)

Let's Pray and We'll Be Done

Have you ever been guilty of using prayer as a tool to corral the kids for at least a minute? It may seem to be the 1 time when all the kids are at least pretending to be respectful. So if you start and end with prayer, at least you get a sense of some order to the small group time. Here are some practical dos and don'ts:

✦ Do write out a prayer every now and then—ahead of time. Think of something specific for each kid that you can put before the Lord.

So You're a Volunteer

If your group is brand spanking new, here's something practical you can do as you start your group: Spend an entire session working with kids to draft a mission statement or letter stating the focus of the group. This will help them set parameters and take ownership of their group values. It also helps them see the bigger picture, and allows them to thrive. This practical exercise can be crucial to achieving their buy-in!

Start with a blank piece of paper and ask the kids to help write basic shared guidelines that will give direction to their group experience. Give them space to share their feelings. Ask questions like, "How should we agree to treat each other when we hang out?" and "Is it our desire to grow by inviting friends, or do we just want to get closer among ourselves?" Ask questions that help them lay out a list of attitudes and agreed-upon traits the group will strive for. Their list should >>

✱ Do take notes in a journal when the kids are talking, and refer to it the next week or at the end of the session in your prayer.

✱ Do pray every now and then with your eyes open, and have your kids open their eyes. Remind them that our God is alive, moving among us when we meet together!

✱ Do find some corporate prayers that your kids can recite aloud.

✱ Do teach Romans 8:26, 27 to your kids. They may not know how to articulate their pain and struggles; they simply need to know that God hears them.

✱ Do appropriately laugh with God. Some things are funny. *Jr. high kids* are funny. It's OK to have a moment in prayer remembering and thanking God for the goofy things that we do that he probably laughs at, too.

✱ Do encourage teens to take on a position of reverence, explaining the connection of the physical and spiritual, since God made both.

✱ Don't ever let prayer time become monotonous, stale, or old hat in any way. Look for creative ways to keep this time fresh.

✱ Don't make it so formal and stiff that kids think God won't hear them if the pastor isn't there to officially intercede on their behalf. Help them memorize Hebrews 4:15, 16.

Open Share Time

Jesus said in Luke 6:45, "The good man brings good things out of the good stored up in his heart, and the evil man brings evil things out of the evil stored up in his heart. For out of the overflow of his heart his mouth speaks" (*NIV*). Our kids have things stored up in their hearts. They are trying to get them out, and it is not always done with words. We have to be ready to listen through every possible avenue.

Chances are that your kids are giving you glaring clues into what they are struggling with. You just need to train your ears to clearly hear. There is a difference between casual chit-chat while hanging out and focused sharing time. Kids want to share, but just telling them 1 time that they can talk to us will not make them do it.

Some small groups do not have this time of sharing because when they have tried to let kids talk, it felt like a miss. We have to build a culture of sharing. When we continually model and promote a safe place to express feelings aloud, kids will come along. Look for ways for all kids to receive safe, unridiculed feedback. Kids give much thought to how their answers will be received by the other kids, so consider these practical tips:

✦ Ask teens to text their answers to you, and pick 1 to expound on.
✦ Encourage teens to journal their answers and then share from those notes if appropriate. Most kids don't have trouble thinking—they

>> include statements that promote a safe environment, privacy, and mutual respect. After you have a list of 10 things that clearly portray a healthy learning environment, ask all the kids to sign the document—displaying their desire to work within boundaries. Then post it somewhere visible. Make copies for each kid. If you've got some kids who are artistic, let them illustrate the mission statement in a visual way, such as by creating a coat of arms. Get out the art supplies and let them go nuts!

just struggle with quickly verbalizing their thoughts. Simply having notes to launch from may give them more confidence.

If introducing jr. high kids to healthy patterns of sharing their feelings with others in the church is the *only* thing that is accomplished during the entire 7th grade year, it was time well spent! Jr. high kids do not have the life experience to know what is appropriate and how to share what is going on in their lives.

This also means that perhaps you'll have to be vulnerable about a specific issue over the course of time with your kids. Clearly there are appropriate boundaries to recognize when sharing, but nothing can beat a real-life example of faith lived out in front of them.

Bringing It Home

People remember 2 things about most experiences. The first is how you start and the second is how you finish. Plan to finish well. Many kids struggle all during small group time to share something, then they finally let it squeak out on the way out the door, just hoping that you catch the anguish or hope in their voices. If we are not alert, we can miss those important moments, and for some kids that might be the only reason they came. I've stood at the door and heard it many times—the mention of a game (in passing) that a kid really wants someone to come and watch, a comment about dreading school, or the anxiety of something waiting at home. Train your ears for the moments when kids open up and let you in. And when it happens, be ready to catch it.

Parents invest huge amounts of time and money in just bringing and picking kids up. They may seem to rush in and out, too busy to stop. Perhaps they feel like they are intruding or not wanted. Prepare for them. Give them a half sheet of paper telling them what was discussed that week or what is coming up. Think about something you can tell each parent about his or her kid if you get the chance. Parents feel alone and scared too—especially if this is their first child! They need to be reminded that you are on their side and pulling for their kids, too.

As you plan to finish each night well, be creative in the way you vary what you do. Here are a few cool ways to end your small group meeting:

* Share group hugs! Appropriate touch is huge. Some kids may come because small group is the only place where they get a healthy, caring touch and word of value spoken to them. Plan it intentionally.
* End your group time in silence for a few minutes 1 week. Tell kids that they can communicate by using motions, but they can't talk. Then lift the ban and enjoy the freedom to communicate and share.
* Invite parents—or other chauffeurs—to a special time of prayer with their kids at the end of small group. Let families know about it ahead of time, and tell parents to come ready to listen to their kids. Facilitate a brief time of communication, affirmation, and sharing.
* Pray over each kid individually. Let the other kids wait for their special turn. Take the time to ask for a special blessing on that specific child's life. Thank God for the unique attributes you see developing in them.
* Play a game of high/low: Ask every teen to name his week's high point and low point. This is a great way to start a prayer time or to get your kids used to speaking in a group setting. It is a primer for more in-depth sharing as they start to elaborate in the high/low game.

Don't Go It Alone

You can't do it all by yourself—prepare for small group each week, think through the snack time, and try to have consistent contact with your kids outside of small group time. If we are calling kids to

So You're in a Small Church

You may need to have high schoolers in the same group with your jr. highers. If so, intentionally designate them as junior leaders in the group. This works well, especially when the content during a given week is intended primarily for the jr. highers. Make sure they know it is important for the jr. high kids to have a safe place to process out loud, free from older teens articulating everything for the group.

join the community of the church, then why would we not model community in our small groups? We all need partners, and none of us has every gift needed to make a small group rock. That is just how God made the church. Don't fight it—embrace it. Jr. high ministry is best when it is shared together.

If you are a college student who relates well with kids, then find a parent to help arrange the rides and snack time for you. If you are an adult who is approaching (or past) midlife, I say props to you for working with jr. highers. Make sure you have some younger adults or college kids on your team to keep you "relevant."

There are many people who can serve but don't because they don't want to be stuck carrying the whole ball, or they don't know what they can offer. They may just be waiting for someone to ask them. Here are some practical ways to get it done:

* Look for other people in your church who would be willing to help you build relationships in small groups by supporting volunteer leaders, coordinating rides and meeting places, and being the bridge for new jr. highers and their parents.
* While some people are better at hanging out and playing basketball and paintball with kids, others are good at baking brownies. Plug people in wherever they fit.
* If you are young in ministry and feel a disconnect between you and the teens' parents, ask a volunteer to be the bridge in communicating and building trust with parents.

Get a team together. Analyze individuals' giftedness, and then give everyone the freedom to do the things at which they excel. Don't be afraid to push one another and let each other grow in new areas, but don't bang your head against the wall when God has equipped the church with every tool it needs to do ministry. We need to be good stewards and harness those tools.

Forming Your Groups

There are many models for doing small groups because our ministry environments are very different. Some churches may have more than 1 type of small group because they have found success in using different methods. Some variables include the type of people resources God has given your church and your meeting space options.

Here are some methods that have been successful with many leaders:

* Have your small groups break out from a main worship service at your church.
* Divide your groups so that they are gender specific.
* Offer a variety of small groups that meet off-site on different nights.
* Allow kids to be in a different small group each week, based on the table they sit at during the main program.
* Organize small groups according to affinities such as playing basketball or cooking.

Putting It All Together

As you start putting the pieces of your small group formula together, don't abandon your methods too soon. Many people plan in detail how to effectively structure small group times for kids.

But too often they don't continually evaluate the process and tweak it where it's consistently not working. Plan to get together with other small group leaders and discuss frustrations or innovations in the game plan. Your goal is to paint a framework of the larger church in which jr. highers can learn to share openly, be accepted, and be challenged to grow. They should see the church as a place that is actively walking them through the developmental crisis of jr. high—a place where they can be themselves.

Whether they have just watched an episode of *Hannah Montana* or played a violent video game, we want to provide the culture in which kids can process holistically what is going on in life from a Christian perspective—something that may be very new to them. Most parents I know *never* circle their kids up after a TV show and help them process it. By the way, on most TV shows parents are depicted as aloof and preoccupied—and when they *do* make an appearance, it is quick and they never really connect with their kids. In real life, kids watch episode after episode of TV without anyone helping them talk about what they are taking in. So getting kids to process out loud may be very foreign to them. It can be awkward at first, but once they experience it, they will grow to love it and so will you.

Assimilate as many volunteers as possible into the small group ministry—but be picky! God has gifted people for certain purposes. If someone is serving in a position that's not right, he's robbing God of 2 things—he is not serving where he should be, and he is taking the space of someone else whom God has called to that position.

Continually evaluate the process with other adult leaders and make changes when necessary. Listen without preconceived notions to the things your kids are saying. Look between the lines to hear the cries of their hearts.

No matter what game plan works best for your situation, 1 thing is for sure: God will work in the hearts of the kids you touch, often behind the scenes. But stand ready for the brilliant "Brittney moments" of glory he will send your way. You don't want to miss them! One of the greatest things about jr. high kids is that they are still enamored with everything in life and can't wait to live it. What a privilege it is for you to hang out with them! I pray that you will make the most of it. ✦

Do This Now

1. How well do you know what is going on in the lives of your teens? The best way to find out the real climate of your group—and get a feel for their needs—is to ask them. Spend a session having them privately answer some survey questions, such as these:
   * Who has hurt someone?
   * Who has destroyed the trust of the group?
   * Who comes to the group because they have to and everyone else knows that?
   * What topics do you think this group should talk about?

2. Revitalize the life of your small group by switching it up with a few of these ideas:
   * Play hooky! Give them a break by ditching the session and playing a game, then share and pray.
   * Do a service project together as a group.
   * Plan a theme night. Everybody loves to dress up. Some possibilities include disco night, pirate and princess night, a theme night based on a current movie, or a pajama party.

* Plan a night to look back. You should constantly be taking pictures! This is a great job for another volunteer who isn't comfortable talking with kids but still has the desire to serve. Maybe you know a parent who would like to be involved and just needs a reason to do so. Photos are needed for every activity, trip, and personal visit. Turn the lights off and show pictures of kids from previous activities and years. Set it to music. Include meaningful verbal or written messages to the kids.
* Have a special banquet. Ask kids to dress up and serve them a nice meal. Celebrate, celebrate, celebrate!

Great Expectations and How to Lower Them

So You Get Paid

As you read this chap-
ter, here are some ques-
tions for you to ponder:
* How are you doing
  at building bridges
  for kids' future crisis
  points?
* Do you know any kids
  right now who are in
  a crisis? Remember
  the presenting
  problem is rarely the
  problem, and the out-
  ward manifestation
  may not be indicative
  of what's going on
  inside.
* When was the last
  time you really did
  something special
  to thank your "glue
  people"? What could
  you do to celebrate
  their unique contribu-
  tions to the jr. high
  ministry?

The process of mentoring kids can be compared to watching 2 people dance. As leaders we want to be successful in our relationships with teens. We have good intentions. We want to make an eternal impact. In the midst of preparing the small group session and hangout time we have expectations concerning how the meeting will go—and what kind of growth will come from it. We expect to see a beautiful dance between 2 individuals in which 1 leads tactically while the other gracefully follows the skillful maneuvers. The leader is exemplifying the right steps, and there have been classes and teaching times on this dance before. It should be a spectacle. Others should see the duo prancing with precision, standing by in astonishment at the fluidity with which the dancers move together. One is leading, the other following—both learning the dance of life together.

We are human, but we can't stop hoping that our time with jr. highers will feel this way. At times we get a taste and see that there are actually a few great moves out there. We get excited because all of this hard work is paying off. We see that some kids have the natural ability to be coached, and we invest heavily in them while still teaching the basics to others. Then right before the big move a kid stops the waltz and starts break dancing—spinning on his head. The other teens quickly join in the fun on the dance floor and the "Electric Slide" breaks out, and then before you know it, there is a full-blown mosh pit!

This is not what you practiced at all. As the instructor you feel it is your duty to make your kids dance the correct steps to the waltz, so you lose composure and forcefully guide them, all the while becoming rigid and awkward in your own dance moves. At times it seems as if both dance partners are falling all over each other. What happened to the days when your partner was so young that he stood on your feet and you held his hands, leading him all the way? Simply put, the jr. high dancers now want to try their own feet and experiment with their own moves. They want to solo instead of group dance. Ministry with jr. high teens is a long road. It is going to take some time.

An Awkward Dance

One of the things I love about working with jr. high kids is their ability to be so moldable. We can teach them some amazing dance moves and they will soar. They will blow our expectations out of the water at how they can move. If we teach them to serve others in Jesus' name, they jump in and invite their friends. They even dare to have fun while serving. They are not ashamed to tell people about their church or relationship with Jesus. At times we stand back and almost feel like they are leading us. What a thrill it is to have the kids we work with seem to completely get what it means to live out their faith.

Perhaps this is just the thing about them that sets us up for disappointment. We come off of a camp week or an awesome Wednesday night meeting, when all of a sudden our dance partners are tripping all over themselves and screwing up everything completely! We should continue to expect the world of them and challenge them like they have no limit, but at the same time be prepared for them to flounder. It is part of the process. One key to having a fulfilling and lasting ministry with jr. highers is to get this principle early on: They can soar, but they *will* make mistakes. Our greatest opportunity is how we react when they do fall.

Their road to spiritual growth is not as linear as we might think. I remember having a definitive call into the ministry in the 6th grade. Beyond a shadow of a doubt I had completely dedicated my life to serving Jesus and his bride, the church, with my vocation. I knew I wanted to go to seminary and prepare myself for ministry, specifically youth ministry. I never walked away from that calling in my heart. But I also frustrated my jr. high leaders when I pushed the lifeguard in the pool at the church swim party . . . apparently not cool. (Sorry about that, Troy!) How could a leader in the youth group do that? I cussed on the football field too, and I even mooned a kid during coed PE . . . outside, in front of a line of elementary school buses . . . full of kids. I spent the next 3 days at "in-school suspension." And the list goes on.

It's not that all these things took away from what the Holy Spirit was continuing to do in my heart. That calling was still a present reality. So was the baggage from my parents' divorce. Working with kids is so much messier than what we desire as leaders. It may look like dance moves are being forgotten and all the instruction we've given didn't take at all.

All Dance Moves Are Not Created Equal

I can't imagine what Bill was thinking when I showed up for our weekly guitar lesson with orange hair. It was the summer after my 7th grade year, and my brothers and I thought we would enjoy the summer being sun gods. That meant getting onto the roof of our house and sunbathing there. I have no idea why we didn't just lie down in the lawn . . . surely it would have been much cooler. Anyway, I decided that I would look like a better guitar player with blond hair, so I put a peroxide product on my hair to lighten it up. By 1:00 in the afternoon it was nowhere near as drastic of a change as I had hoped for, so I applied additional doses for the rest of the afternoon—thus the orange hair. My stepmom refused to let me cut my hair that summer. I was called Ronald McDonald the whole next week at camp.

I didn't color my hair because I was rebelling or because there was some covered-up issue that I needed to talk out. The truth was that I was a goofy kid, and we all laughed about that story that summer . . . and every summer since. The other truth was that I missed my real mother and wondered what it would be like to live with her every day. There is always *another* story. We have to listen to what is not being said. In this dance with kids there are always opportunities to build a bridge and connect on a deeper level of trust.

Don't Freak Out, Because Right Now I Am

Brenda built bridges over and over again. There was no specific instance that stood out as the moment when I knew she was trustworthy. Brenda was a volunteer leader in my group who simply showed up consistently every week. She played cards with us, watched us play basketball, and was the best big sister ever! She clicked with us because she danced very well—by listening to us and participating in the things that were meaningful to us. She remembered when our games were happening and did her best to attend them. Brenda was also very good at bringing other adults into the picture.

I like to describe people like Brenda as glue. Every great jr. high ministry has to have "glue people." They make the other adults and kids just glad to be a part of something so cool. Because Brenda put the work in, she reaped the blessing of many crisis moments. Kids seemed to gravitate toward Brenda when their moments of despair surfaced.

Kids are constantly testing the water with adults. We might think they are joking about something when in fact they are really giving us a picture of what is going on in their hearts. Brenda picked up on those kinds of things and would dig deeper. She passed the tests all the time.

Brenda lived with her mother just down the road from me. I remember showing up at their house one night a mess. My father and stepmother were blending a family together of 4 boys. We were within 4 years of each other, and there were difficult times. Brenda and her mom just listened. They didn't freak out. They served me iced tea, talked, and sent me home on my bike with hope.

Crisis times are going to come. We only have a few opportunities to lay the groundwork that is so necessary for these moments. Have I said this yet? Kids *will* make mistakes—hopefully not *huge* ones. And when they do make those mistakes, we want them to view us as a safe place to process what may be the underlying issue. We are building a bridge for a crisis point in the future. We simply cannot let the time for teaching obstruct the reality of what our kids are currently living, trying, and feeling.

Relax, It's Not on You

This chapter flies in the face of many unfortunate perspectives that people have about jr. high kids. Too many people expect them to dance in a proper fashion all the time, forgetting that there is a learning curve for those growing into their bodies. The kids in your community are a gift from the Father and they should not be avoided like the plague during the difficult jr. high years. God thinks they are pretty special. Psalm 127:3 shows us God's perspective on children: "Sons are a heritage from the LORD, children a reward from him" (*NIV*). And Proverbs 17:6 says, "Children's children are a crown to the aged, and parents are the pride of their children" (*NIV*).

We need all hands on deck to dance with kids! They are complex and make no sense at times. One minute they soar and the next they crash and burn. They are experimenting; they are finding out who they are. It is a difficult trial-and-error period in life. Sometimes kids need to borrow some hope from us after they have failed. Their mistakes do not make up their whole person—and it is not all on us to help them figure out the dance of life.

In Acts 16 the apostle Paul was preaching on a riverbank near Philippi. He met a woman there who listened to his teachings. Just like many of the lessons you have struggled through during your small group, Paul was simply teaching. I receive encouragement by reading verse 14: "As she listened to us, the Lord opened her heart, and she accepted what Paul was saying."

We are not alone as we teach kids. When they make mistakes and we feel like it is all on us or we have failed them—we are not alone. Our God pursues the hearts and minds of our kids. It is the Holy Spirit who will open their hearts to his message. Our job is to simply

So You're in a Small Church

Help your kids see that while their church is small, God's kingdom is big—just as he is! Look for the hand of God moving all over the world, and then point that out to your teens. Perhaps you have just 2 to 4 kids in your jr. high age group. You can do many things a larger group can't do that demonstrate the bigness of God and make an impact on others. Pick up your kids for a quick service project and ice cream. Invite them to serve in the church alongside older people on a weekly basis. Be encouraged—small means you have the opportunity to have a greater and deeper impact!

be obedient to the task of Psalm 78:4—telling the next generation "the praiseworthy deeds of the Lord" (*NIV*). And if we live long enough, even though getting on the dance floor may be difficult for us, we will derive great joy from watching the next generation carry on the dance. ✦

Do This Now

1. Ask the Holy Spirit to help you see when something is a big deal and needs attention or when you just need to laugh.

2. Stretch out and chill . . . no, seriously. It's not by your power, knowledge, or ability that jr. high kids are ultimately changed. It is by your obedience to God's Word in pointing them to him that starts, perpetuates, and closes the deal!

3. Fight the urge to label kids. They watch how we deal with other kids. It tells them how we will treat them in a similar situation. Model a culture of listening, loving, and forgiving.

4. Realize that despair is despair. Don't rate a kid's level of hurt based on your perception of it. What may seem trivial to you can be life-altering to a young teen. Trust that it is a big deal, and give them the benefit of the doubt.

5

Get Out of the Way!

Do you remember the famous scene in *The Karate Kid* when Daniel was working for Mr. Miyagi? Daniel thought he was going to be learning Chuck Norris-like roundhouse kicks expressed with low, guttural inflections. But instead, he felt like Mr. Miyagi was simply getting free labor out of him. Daniel eventually blew up and confronted his new sensei about his teaching methods. It was at this critical moment that we discovered that Daniel had been learning things all along that had real-life implications. He had received much usable information. The time was not yet right for the special "crane kick" move, but the "wax on, wax off" preparation was an all-important part of the learning process.

This is how your teens may feel at times. They may simply see themselves painting a fence, or waxing on and then waxing off. In actuality, all the small group sessions, relationships, and work they are putting into their faith are preparing them for a crash course with reality. We are trying to earn the opportunity to speak into their lives at a pivotal point. All of our efforts spent investing in and mentoring them are building a relational bridge. Our prayer is that God will go before us and prepare the catalytic conversations in his perfect time. What a blessing this is! We don't have to be superhuman—just accessible. Our availability to kids in a consistent and healthy environment creates a place for them to develop their own lasting faith.

Don't Measure with the Wrong Ruler

As I work with jr. high kids, 1 word that continually comes to mind is *surprise*. When I talk with small group leaders at the end of summer camp or the end of a school year, I am constantly amazed by the stories I hear—stories about the change that is taking place in kids' lives. One of the great joys of working with kids is that they are not like us. Change comes much easier for them. We forget this from time to time and get blown away by what suddenly comes to the surface. The story line usually goes something like this: "I had no idea that he was feeling or processing any of this stuff, and then he just burst open with all these thoughts and huge statements!"

One kid shares and you ask if anyone else identifies with the subject at hand, and the most unlikely of kids will be completely engaged at a deep level. It's so surprising because everything on the outside says that the teen is uninterested, bored, and dreaming of playing video games—that he is being forced to come to small group.

Young adolescents don't have much practice in showing emotions and communicating effectively about what they're going through. They may not understand that they are going through a situation that is temporary, so their struggle is troubling them on an even deeper level. Just because they can't say it does not mean that they are not feeling or thinking about it on the inside.

Give Them Time

Jr. high small groups are intensely dynamic. In the same group there can be a very wide gap in the cognitive abilities of various kids. What seems random in a particular kid's understanding and behavior could be attributed to any number of major developments that have captured the better part of his concentration (either

So You Get Paid

As you digest this chapter, here are some additional questions for you to think about:

* How are you doing at giving your teens room to think and process? What evidence do you see that tells you that they are working out the content on a deeper level?

* As the teens learn to process on their own, do you see any frustration building up in your volunteers? In what ways can you encourage them to be patient and wait on God's timing?

* What specific measures tell you that certain teens are adopting faith principles as their own?

consciously or subconsciously). While kids are at a transitional phase in cognitive developmental ability, they should still be pushed to explore higher thinking models involving abstract thought. It is not that they are completely incapable of thinking with these new skills, but they will be novices and will need extra time to experience abstract thinking.

Educators realize that there is a shift in what is crucial developmentally for jr. high kids during early adolescence. "The period of academic slowdown that occurs . . . must be considered in the development of learning materials. This . . . means that they should not be pushed beyond their academic capabilities during these years. For the majority of kids, early adolescence is not a time for great academic strides. One of the most important goals of middle-level education is to have early adolescents make significant strides in personal and social development as they become young adults. Thus, during the middle grades, academics must be balanced with affective educational concerns."[3]

This is great news because the church can take its rightful place in helping kids learn about how God made them—and the world—in a holistic fashion. Instead of shying away from discussions with kids about abstract ideas, we need to keep in mind their developmental stage and give them room to breathe. We must do our best to guard against showing frustration and impatience. Do the kids you work with trust you not to walk ahead of them but *with them* as they grow? If they do not trust you, they will retreat to an underworld where you will most likely not be invited.

You Do Your Part, So That He Can Do His

Kids explore a gamut of emotions because they are exploring the depth of the human experience. While the feelings and understanding at the time of emotional outpouring are genuine, it's important to bring those encounters back up in discussion later. Revisit their thoughts with them on a different day. Help kids process their thoughts and emotions so that through them they feel a connection with God. Kids will participate in a public prayer, communion service, or other traditions of faith authentically, but they need to be walked through the rest of the story. The small group experience can help them connect the dots. They need to be prompted to rethink the experience outside of the church. Practicing this over and over, in new places and from new perspectives, helps to cultivate in them a system for thinking about God and inviting him into every part of their lives. You might need to celebrate the brokenness a teen feels on a Thursday night at camp, then ask him over for a soda a month later and help him walk through what that moment meant at camp . . . and what it means to him now.

Ultimately we have to realize that God is pursuing the hearts and minds of our kids. No doubt you love them and can be a tool in God's hand to impact them, but the loving Father is doing the real work in their lives. Ask yourself this question from time to time: "Am I cluttering up what God wants to do and getting in his way, or am I more concerned with waiting on him, listening, and being available?"

Strive to cultivate an environment where ideas about faith and God's Word are meditated on over time. That means that you may not have a tidy conclusion at the end of small group each week . . . or even at the end of a study series. Keep bringing up the topic. Kids are hurried in so many aspects of their

So You're in a Small Church

You may live in a small town where everybody knows everybody's business. This may be especially true at church. If your teens are dealing with some dysfunction in their homes, it won't be very hard for you to "stay out of the way." But, be available if they need you. You might be more of a lifeline than you know. Look for opportunities where you can lift up, praise, and help a teen who is wrestling with something—even if it is messy.

lives. Church and the small group experience should provide them a place to *not* be hurried. What is God's nature when it comes to giving people time to process life? He is patient. Meditate on these verses and the impact they can have on your jr. high small group:

- "The Lord is compassionate and merciful, slow to get angry and filled with unfailing love. He will not constantly accuse us, nor remain angry forever. He does not punish us for all our sins; he does not deal harshly with us, as we deserve" (Psalm 103:8-10).
- "I knew that you are a merciful and compassionate God, slow to get angry and filled with unfailing love. You are eager to turn back from destroying people" (Jonah 4:2).
- "The Lord isn't really being slow about his promise, as some people think. No, he is being patient for your sake. He does not want anyone to be destroyed, but wants everyone to repent" (2 Peter 3:9).

Jr. High Kids Rock

Sara reminds me of just how difficult it is to be patient and get out of the way. Sara was Cherry's little sister. Cherry always shared in small group time and seemed to be developing her own faith deeply throughout her jr. high years. As Sara moved into the jr. high ministry, she attended and participated willingly in every aspect of it. Sara was not what adults would label a "leader" in the confines of the church, but she was polite and generally flew under the radar. With friends at church she was always at the center of something funny and was very well-liked. At school, Sara excelled in sports and academics—and her lively spirit made her very popular.

I worried that she was going through the motions in her faith and that peer pressure at school would ultimately guide her away from her family's faith. I specifically remember watching her at camp one summer as she just seemed to glide through the activities and didn't seem to be getting the whole point of it all. I was frustrated and mentioned it to her sister Cherry. I just knew Sara was headed for big trouble. I spoke with my wife about my concerns. I felt compelled to sit Sara down and unload all my wisdom on her, from the perspective of a caring adult, of course.

Cherry was the oldest girl of 3 siblings. Sara was the youngest, and I made the mistake, I am sure, of labeling her the carefree, clueless, wild baby of the family. Their brother had never been to church that much, which only compounded my fear for Sara. The week of camp passed, and for some reason I never did sit down and attempt to shake her up.

Sara went on to become the captain of the cheerleading team in her high school years and was considered by all to be a member of the "in crowd." Despite her many accomplishments at school and in her social life, she continued to be involved in ministry at church. During Christmas break of Sara's senior year she hosted a party at her home for a group of her senior friends. Through other kids in our ministry, I heard the whole story and the consequences Sara would reap from the choices she had

So You're a Volunteer

Hey, you may be better at this patience thing than the paid youth pastor or jr. high professional. He's probably feeling the pressure to produce changed lives. What can you do to encourage him or her? Also spend some time thinking about the "Saras" within your sphere of influence. Ask God to help you achieve the right balance between knowing when to gently push, when to just listen, and when to get out of the way and let God take over.

made that night. It was no secret in the school. Every teen knew what happened and how the rest of her senior year would then play out.

Sara told Cherry ahead of time about her intentions to tell her best friends about who Jesus is and what he meant to her. She gathered the kids in the family living room and told them her story. She invited them to share their stories as well. The party ended abruptly. There was a consensus among the senior class to treat Sara as an outcast. She was not only to be ignored, but also to be treated with contempt. At basketball games for the rest of the season, Sara would start and finish cheers, and then the other girls would huddle opposite her like hens ritualizing strict pecking orders. It was a difficult 3 months until her graduation. In the midst of this tough situation for Sara, some of the "in crowd" kids decided to attend our Sunday night outreach program. Sara's actions had a profound impact and compelled some kids to wrestle with their own faith on a deeper level. Ultimately, 2 of Sara's closest girlfriends came to know and believe in Jesus over the course of the next year.

To this day, I believe that it would have been a huge mistake for me to have a discussion with Sara during the week of summer camp. There were things I could have said that would have been helpful, but I was not in the right frame of mind. It would have been an unhealthy distraction from what God was doing. *I* wanted Sara to act a certain way to affirm our ministry and my work. *Jesus* wanted to be the Lord of her life. God's *better* is always better. His better always brings the glory to him, not to us.

What about it? Have you ever gotten in the way of what God is doing? If God is patient toward us, how can we do anything less than to extend the same patience to the kids with whom we've been entrusted? We are called to simply do our part in obedience and trust that God is working in the teens whose bodies, minds, and emotions are changing at record speeds. ✦

Do This Now

1. Fight the urge to "fix" kids. They can smell an adult who has an agenda to fix them. They want someone to walk with them.

2. Be honest with kids about an issue that is taking you awhile to figure out.

3. Think back over a big transformation in your life. While there may have been mountaintops and defining moments, that journey was likely more a season of reflection than 1 small group session.

4. Take yourself out of the equation. Your teens' ability to arrive at a certain answer quickly is not a reflection of your skill. It's about them, not us.

5. Memorize a Bible verse that speaks of God's patience toward you.

Parents Are #1

When school let out in Indiana at 2:36, it took Bethany about 14 minutes to come bopping into our youth staff offices, commandeer my computer, and plop her book bag on what was her after-school desk. (Just so you know, other staff members were around and our office was a very safe environment.) I didn't mind because that was ministry—lots of kids would come to hang out for a few hours after school at my office.

Bethany was a typical latchkey kid. Her mother was single, and her dad hadn't been in the picture for as long as Bethany could remember. She started her search for her father on my computer. In those days, the Internet was just becoming a tool where things like that could happen. Bethany's mom loved her hanging out at the church building and even came with her on Sundays from time to time.

I watched Bethany's mom pass through several parenting styles during Bethany's time in our jr. high small group. She went from a season of being disengaged, to being passive, and then to a brief time as an authoritarian. Much of her style depended upon the harsh reality of being a working single mom. Bethany's mom made some mistakes that would have been easy to point out to Bethany. She was an at-risk kid. Many interactions with her mom led to a point of frustration for Bethany, and Bethany often asked us to be a solutions provider. In her mom's mind, we were there to fix her kid, or at least keep her out of trouble—after all, that is what we got paid for, right? Put this on the back burner. I'll return to Bethany's story later.

Many youth leaders get into youth ministry because they click better with kids than they do with adults. To those individuals, it often comes as a surprise just how much adult ministry is still involved in working with kids. We desire to make use of the right tools and methods that can be a catalyst for life change in the kids we work with. But we must understand this fact: In spite of all our good intentions and education concerning the development of jr. high kids, nothing can derail or skyrocket the faith of a teen more than the involvement of a parent. If you are a parent leading a small group, I encourage you to read this chapter with a heart open to the leading of the Holy Spirit. If you don't have kids of your own yet, you especially need to read with an honest and open heart.

God knit together and specially ordained the institution of the family to raise children. He even drew a picture of what this is supposed to look like during the ebb and flow of life: "My son, obey your father's commands, and don't neglect your mother's instruction. Keep their words always in your heart. Tie them around your neck. When you walk, their counsel will lead you. When you sleep, they will protect you. When you wake up, they will advise you. For their command is a lamp and their instruction a light; their corrective discipline is the way to life" (Proverbs 6:20-23).

So You Get Paid

As you read this chapter, consider your answers to the following:
* Where on the continuum would you currently place your attitude toward the parents of the teens in your ministry?

Affirming |———————+———————+———————+———————+ Antagonistic

* What practical things could you do to move more toward the affirming side?
* Have you ever made mistakes in relating to a parent for which you need to repent and ask for forgiveness? Are you currently in danger of hurting a relationship with a parent because of your perspective? What can you do to help heal the situation?

Spend some time looking at the parenting style chart on page 76 and thinking about the following questions.
* What parenting style does your youth ministry and small group model most resemble?
* What model do various volunteers in your ministry gravitate towards? Do you know why?
* What strengths and weaknesses of your model do you need to talk about with your leadership team?

All of our methodology and programs can do great good working with the family unit—or great harm if we do not approach our task by seeing God's perspective concerning the role of parents in spiritual transformation. Many youth ministries are hindered in effectiveness and their leaders lose support from the church because of issues dealing with parents. Research currently shows that even when parents don't feel like they count, they still are the largest contributing factor to the spiritual formation of their jr. high kids.

You Are Not the #1 Influencer

By simply glancing at our ability to control and manipulate what a small group thinks is cool, we may think we have a great influence. Kids seem to tell us that they think we are great, and we even get the feeling that they look up to us as their small group leaders. But don't be fooled. We have an amazing opportunity to model faith and impact kids, walking them through what could be the most difficult years of their young lives, but their parents ultimately set the most likely course for their system of beliefs. Even though parents themselves may try to toss the baton and label volunteer youth workers as the greatest influence, they still wield the number 1 spot. At the end of the day, parents are the real front lines to the formation of their own kids' identity.

We get the opportunity to put our own 2 cents in at small group. Perhaps we have invested more on a relational level with certain kids, in attending their events and meeting their friends. Teens are viewing our information about faith through the lens of their most dominant social context—a group of peers. That is the one where they spend the most time and can have, in their minds, the most drastic impact on their immediate reality. But no matter what level of influence we have on them, we carry nowhere near the weight of even a disengaged parent.

We are not the only ones fooled into thinking that parents no longer have the number 1 influence in a kid's life. Parents themselves have been duped. Some parents no longer remember (or have never heard) God's Word in Deuteronomy 6: "These commandments that I give you today are to be upon your hearts. Impress them on your children. Talk about them when you sit at home and when you walk along the road, when you lie down and when you get up. Tie them as symbols on your hands and bind them on your foreheads. Write them on the doorframes of your houses and on your gates" (vv. 6-9, *NIV*). To many kids today, this might sound like nagging or hounding. But to me, impressing something on a child sounds more hands-on than simply hoping or pointing in the right direction.

When a parent begins to believe that he or she has no influence, the parent may stop trying. Parents pull back and believe they have done all they can and then act as bystanders with really good seats. They may continue to speak up, but only when they feel a big issue warrants it. Frustration and fear set in. It is as if parents have given up their God-appointed obligation to speak into their kids' lives (Ephesians 6:1-4).

Still not sure if parents are the number 1 influencer in a kid's life? In 2002–03 the National Survey of Youth and Religion (NSYR) conducted some significant research. Over the course of a year the NSYR completed a national, random-digit-dial telephone survey of U.S. households containing at least 1 teenager (ages 13–17). Then they followed up with more extensive in-depth, face-to-face interviews of 267 families from 45 states that represented a broad range of difference among teens in religion, age, race, sex, socioeconomic status, rural-suburban-urban residence, region of the country, and language spoken. The chart below was a part of their findings.[4]

Association of the Importance of Faith in Daily Life for U.S. Parents of Teenagers and of Their Adolescent Children, Ages 13–17 (Row percentages)

	Teen Importance of Faith					
Parent Importance of Faith	Extremely	Very	Somewhat	Not Very	Not at All	% Total
Extremely important	30	37	24	5	3	100
Very important	14	32	36	12	5	100
Fairly important	7	23	38	21	10	100
Somewhat important	8	15	41	20	16	100
Not very important	3	11	37	22	26	100
Not important at all	2	15	37	19	28	100

Source: National Survey of Youth and Religion, 2002–3.

The percentage of teens who have a belief system that directly aligns with that of their parents is quite large. Of parents who reported that their faith is extremely important in their daily lives, 67 percent of their teens reported that faith is *extremely important* or *very important* in their daily lives. Only 8 percent of those parents' teens reported that faith is *not very* or *not at all* important in their lives. Kids with parents not possessing a faith that they view as important rarely swing to the opposite end of the spectrum. The table shows drastically low numbers of kids swinging in either direction, vastly different from their parents. More disturbing yet is the pattern where numbers show kids taking their cues from parents for whom faith *is not important at all*. It doesn't matter what we hope kids will turn out to be; what matters most is the context in which they grow up.

3 Key Issues

As they develop, teens struggle with 3 dominant issues: identity, autonomy, and affinity. The process of their identity (forming concepts of who they are and how they fit into adult society) comes together as they explore both autonomy ("I am going places on my own and getting a sense of who I could become on my own") and affinity ("What groups do I belong to, and how do those groups shelter, protect, and define who I am becoming?").

Concerning autonomy, many kids experiment with multiple versions of their identity and what they might do to get there. Just because they are dressing a certain way or emulating a personality they have seen does not necessarily mean they like it themselves. They desire a sense of independence and all outward signs show that they have no inhibitions about it—but they may be very afraid underneath the exterior.

Some of their affinity groups may be in direct conflict with each other. We should not assume that a young teen is ideologically sold out to any group with whom he aligns himself. Some of the reasons they are in such groups might be obscure, trivial, and fleeting; or they might indicate real interest and future direction. When kids feel like they belong somewhere, everything else falls into place. And that is where the small group experience can make a significant impact in their impressionable lives. Affinity can be a powerful tool in the small group dynamic. The urge to feel connected with meaning and value is an unexplainable core drive in the minds of all teens.

And when this is not successfully realized, kids can take massive developmental steps backward, and intense trauma can occur—causing a series of hurtful experiences that could take years to overcome. (But hey, no pressure!)

On the positive side, teens who feel a sense of belonging can develop at an amazing speed. Over the years, there seem to be shifts in how kids may express 1 of these 3 issues (identity, autonomy, and affinity) more than others. Most kids don't have a problem revealing their emotions in an outward manner. Movies have demonstrated to kids that it is healthy to express their individual voices through their identity, autonomy, and affinity groups. Unfortunately it doesn't always turn out exactly the same way in real life.

During my formative jr. high years, I started the school year at new schools 3 years in a row. I learned some painful and valuable lessons during each of those new ventures. Moving from a metro Denver area school to a small town in Indiana tested my resolve for identity. In my mind I was mimicking what I perceived to be quite normal—and normal was what was I saw on TV, right? A vivid out-of-body video still plays in my head of day 1 of 7th grade at Paul Hadley Middle School. I see myself with a tightly wound Kirk Cameron, mullet-like perm, walking down the halls. I had hijacked one of my father's pink *Miami Vice* shirts. It really looked like I had wrestled with and killed a pink flamingo. My stonewashed jeans with holes in them were a sight, but nothing topped my dangling fire bolt earring! (My uncle had gotten me jazzed about the symbolism of God sending Satan to roam the earth on a lightning bolt from Heaven.) Let's just say that my explanation didn't play very well in Peoria!

Isn't that classic? You probably have a version of my former self in your group today. He wants autonomy and validation of his individuality, but it isn't playing out the way he thinks it is. Coming of age is tough business and if anyone makes it through adolescence without a story like mine, he was robbed of some jr. high milestones.

As parents react to what they see in their teens' lives, they play a huge role in what their kids are becoming. Without Christ as a part of an adolescent's search in these areas, some level of dissatisfaction will be apparent.

So You're Not a Parent Yourself

* Be encouraged that you are not totally dumb on the subject just because you don't have your own kids. You can still study kids, hang with them, listen, and stand on the ground of your personal investment in specific teens. Also know that the Holy Spirit is guiding you.

* Be willing to listen to parents; that gesture alone will win you credibility.

* Understand that trust can take some time to build—so be patient.

* Think about why you are working with kids. God puts people into positions of leadership. If God affirms that he has you in your position to serve, then be confident in the fact that you are being obedient to him.

* Work with parents to understand their kids' commitments. When they participate in extracurricular activities, they understand that practice is part of the deal. What happens when kids decide—with or without parental endorsement—to pursue their faith deeper? What does spiritual practice look like for a jr. high kid? If being a part of band means going to school, warming up, rehearsing music, getting instruction on technique, and practicing more at home, what should practicing faith in Jesus look like? You can gently help parents understand this.

Then What About Us?

If parents so clearly have a stronghold on what a child's belief system will be, why then do we volunteer, sacrifice, and scrap for the hearts of those kids? While parents are the most significant influencers, they are not the *only* influencers. Kids who have parents who are strong believers need to grow into their own faith. We get to be a part of that. And there *is* a small percentage of kids who drastically break free from a family system in which Christ is not in control. In the NSYR study quoted earlier, several contributing factors in reaching kids whose parents had no system of beliefs included the following: a youth worker's involvement, and 5 or more friends who had a belief system.[5] The good news is that small groups can be the difference maker. Wow! I hope you are celebrating that fact with me. Could it be inferred that the number of teens from non-Christian homes who come to Christ is low because we do not have enough faith-based small groups? What you are doing with your small group is the dynamic that can bring about life change in a teen whose parent does not believe! Let me say that again. *What you are doing with your small group is the dynamic that can bring about life change in a teen whose parent does not believe!* Get your head around that.

As we seek to influence kids' lives, we need to move them from having an antagonistic attitude toward their parents to a more affirming one. In order to effectively partner with them, we must seek to get inside their skin. And, in doing so, it is helpful to be aware of different kinds of parental styles. What parenting methods are the teens in your small group experiencing at home? I am indebted to Christian Smith for the following chart on parent styles.

Key Factors

1. Strong & clear expectations, boundaries, demands, accountability

		HIGH	LOW
2. Emotional warmth, closeness	HIGH	Authoritative!	Permissive
	LOW	Authoritarian	Disengaged

All kids need a mix of both factors in order to really flourish. They need strong and clear expectations, boundaries, demands, and accountability coupled with emotional warmth and closeness. The best approach for healthy child development is a high blend of these factors. As your teens learn to trust you, at some point it might be a good exercise to help them think through their parents' most dominant styles. That will help inform you about what kind of specialized approaches will work best with each kid in the small group setting. Think about the kids in your group, and ask yourself the following questions:

✦ What concepts would each teen easily get (or not comprehend at all) because of his or her experience at home?
✦ What views of God do kids have a natural inclination to sway toward because of their context at home?

- Do they see God as disengaged, with low expectations of him and no real intimacy?
- Do they see God as all about rules with little display of tenderness?

Check Your Page Number

If you really want to know where a kid is coming from, get in his home. A close audit of each teen's context is critical to assessing how to best minister to him. Are you on the same page as the parents of your teens? In respect to their faith, what wishes do parents have for the teens with whom you work? You cannot assume that because parents regularly attend church or profess a high importance in faith that their wishes for their teens' faith development align with yours. Imagine the difficulty a kid has in processing Jesus' call to a radical faith while his parent really only wants his child to stay out of trouble and learn some good manners. (Of course we also want our small group members to stay out of trouble . . . but manners are relative with jr. high kids!)

There is a huge chasm between calling kids to follow God wherever he sends them and the dominant message of society that tells them to simply have fun at whatever they do—but not to fail. Are the parents of your jr. highers assuming that you are giving their kids a version of religion that is simply therapeutic in nature? As you take an inventory of the context in which your kids find themselves, your teaching times and moments spent in their lives will only deepen your insight into what lies beneath the face they put on. You may now start to celebrate huge victories with them and their parents that might have been brushed over before. And God may be doing some great things in the life of the whole family that you only have an inkling about. Do your best to get on *his* page!

Partnering with Parents

When we try to take over and step into the role as the number 1 influencer in kids' lives, we are making it about ourselves. Our greatest role might be to advocate on behalf of parents with their kids. Encourage parents to take back the initiative to speak into the lives of their kids even when their offspring act like they don't care. Encourage parents to stay with it and to push through. Constantly impress upon them that their words carry the heaviest influence on their kids' decisions. Think about some ways in which you can dialogue with them about their involvement in their kids' faith formation.

There is an identity-defining relationship between a parent and a child. Even in the case of a deceased parent or a parent who is not present for other various reasons, the memory of that person has a profound identity-shaping power on a child. Look for some cool things in your teens that you know they inherited from their parents—and when the opportunity presents itself, affirm the parents for this. This will put a happy smile on their faces, and it may just make their day—or their week!

Some Lessons Learned

Remember Bethany? My wife and I had a significant impact on her life during her jr. high years. While on vacation a year ago, we met with Bethany 2,000 miles from where we first nurtured her in small group. Our meeting that day was symbolic of the long road she had traveled since our investment in her life. While I played with our kids on the playground, Bethany walked my wife through her story since early adolescence. She recounted some joys and sorrows—the adventure of helping to plant a church, the trauma of losing a child at birth, the pain of going through a divorce. Her mom had been through some good times and difficult ones as well. The relationship between mother and daughter had encountered some rocky spots, but it was still intact.

Of all the kids whose lives we had an impact on through small groups in jr. high, I would rank our relationship with Bethany near the top. We shared the road with her. She was part of our story in a meaningful way. She reminded us why we believe in jr. high ministry.

But as I look back now, I wish I had affirmed Bethany's mom more and had encouraged her to talk to her daughter in some healthy ways. I wish we had encouraged her to be more proactive in giving input into Bethany's life. Even when she felt guilty or not good enough to speak up, I should have pushed her to do so anyway, because Bethany was never going to look her mom in the eye and

If You're Having Conflict with a Parent

* Know the laws in your state.
* Defuse the situation, as best you can.
* Keep the teen out of it as much as possible.
* Realize that the teens are watching your actions and that they perceive more than you imagine.
* Practice the principles found in Matthew 18:15, 16. They apply in youth ministry, too!
* Record the journey in a journal. This will help you look back and see God at work. It can also serve as evidence in your defense, if necessary.
* Never give up on a parent, because their kid never will.
* Find some common ground. For instance, a parent may not want to endorse your stance on Jesus being the only way to Heaven, but he does want good things and good choices for his kid. Allow him to join you in advocating commonly held interests. Affirm his right to speak into his child's life even when his child may act like he is not listening. You may be winning ground in a relationship that will turn into an opportunity to share Jesus with that parent.
* Remember that parents may be afraid. Fear can cause people to react in strange ways. Anything you can do to reassure a parent, de-escalate a situation, and offer perspective will be appreciated by both teens and parents.

say she forgave her for all the things that had brought about some of their problems. She was never going to say, "Mom, just spend some time with me and tell me your story; tell me what you were like when you were my age." Bethany was going to roll her eyes and hole up in her room when, and if, her mom was home.

Life took my family away from Bethany shortly after her high school years. Bethany's mom was still there, though. Disengaged or passive, she was there—influencing Bethany's identity, whether intentionally or not. One of our greatest roles as small group leaders is not only to help kids see Christ in our example, but also to help parents reclaim their proper role in modeling Christ. I confess that I pushed her mom out of my plan for ministering to Bethany. I didn't have time to work with her mom because she seemed too far gone. I now feel that I didn't open my mind up to what God could have done. I missed some opportunities to connect with Bethany's mom and create bridges to affirm her. Admittedly, waiting on her mom and involving her would have been way messier. But the conversation with Bethany at the park years later may have been different had I realized years earlier that her mom was the number 1 influencer in her life.

Part of the Process

Some in our culture are pushing us to believe that only specialists should work with kids and that parents really don't understand them. I strongly believe that parents need to reengage—and we can help in that process. Today's teens are being hurried through adolescence and are being left to their own conclusions on all sorts of topics without adults to help them discover healthy habits for processing their changing lives. Adults are often viewed as mere facilitators, not allowed into the tightly-knit social teen world. The church is the last institution that exists in which kids can get to know someone from a different generation outside their home. Small groups help introduce other adults into their lives.

Holistic small group ministry always keeps in mind a parent's perspective in what is ultimately in the best interest of a teen. The apostle Paul said, "And I am certain that God, who began the good work within you, will continue his work until it is finally finished on the day when Christ Jesus returns" (Philippians 1:6). How awesome it is that we get to be part of the process of what God is doing in the lives of jr. highers! ✦

Do This Now

1. Never destroy a parent's credibility in front of his or her teen unless the issue at hand will bring harm to the child.

2. When you must choose between gaining the kid's trust or the parent's trust in a situation, take the win with the parent. The kid will thank you . . . much later in life. Sorry, that's just the nature of the beast.

3. Encourage parents to tell stories about their lives to their kids. Rarely will kids ask a parent to do this, though they really want to know their parents' stories. These are, in fact, part of their stories, too.

4. Communicate in ways that parents appreciate most. Don't assume just because you sent an e-mail blast or sent a paper home with their kids that they are informed and will click their heels at attention. Search out what form of communication works best for them. Ask, listen, and adjust accordingly. Responding to their needs can make a huge difference in building bridges of trust.

5. Ask yourself this question from time to time: How are parents invited into the process of your jr. high ministry? What are you saying by omission?

7

Making Friends

Certain events in youth ministry stand out in our memories above others. I remember 1 such special night. Periodically we designed a service where kids would be given tactile ways to encourage one another in non-threatening ways. If you've ever done the exercise where you have 1 kid sit in the center of the circle and then have everyone else encourage him, and after 9 sincere "thanks for being cool" comments you've ended the activity, then you know what I mean. In an effort to help kids have a meaningful exchange with each other, we handed out cheap pages of little stickers and asked kids to give stickers to other kids that either signified a blessing to them or represented something they appreciated about them. Everyone received different colors of stickers, and while the band played we announced a time to hand out a certain color, explaining the meaning behind gifting that sticker to another teen.

Stacey had a bubbly personality and was never afraid to be kind to anyone at anytime. Before Twitter existed, Stacey was the girl you'd only have to tell something to, and you could be assured that everyone else would know what was going on. Some kids called Stacey annoying, obnoxious, and loud. Regardless, she was a real friend to many kids during their dark hours. At one point during our gifting of stickers, a leader in our group asked all the kids in the room to raise their hands if they had ever come to a church activity because Stacey had gone out of her way to simply invite them. For Stacey, it was a defining and rewarding moment for being a true friend. She wanted her friends to hear about Jesus, and she knew that it would happen if she could get them to come. For me, it was incredible to see the power of friendship, as more than half of the 200 kids in our youth room raised their hands.

Kids' friendships make a great impact—both positive and negative—on small group dynamics. We can't control it, but if we can learn how to roll with the punches, there's hope that there can be more positives than negatives.

There is no shortage of options of events, clubs, and after-school activities for kids to involve themselves in. We often feel like we are fighting for our spot in the busy lives of jr. high teens. Just as all the physical and emotional development in jr. highers is reaching a crescendo, the influx of a heightened sense to their social world compounds the pressure. We can easily get lost in the shuffle if we don't take a larger view of our small group's collective spiritual journey. Suddenly, surprises pop up in the form of friends. We spend all kinds of time investing in the kids in our small group, their parents, and getting to know their unique context—then out of nowhere they show up talking and dressing completely differently than they used to, and they're mentioning the name of someone we have never heard before.

The social world of an early adolescent is volatile. The innate desire for a sense of belonging is so great that kids spend vast amounts of

So You Get Paid

As you read this chapter, think about the following:
* These are perhaps the 2 most practical bits of wisdom I've ever heard concerning jr. high ministry:
  1. Don't swim with your jr. high kids and their friends. They will literally drown you and not even know it . . . or care!
  2. End lock-ins at 12:01 AM. Nothing good ever happens after 12:01 (according to my mom). Eighty percent of the win can be realized from 6:00 PM to 12:01. Your parents, volunteers, and the church elders will thank you.
* If you haven't done so in awhile, evaluate the pros and cons of your philosophy for jr. high small groups in your church. Do you have open or closed groups, or do you have a combination of both? What are the strengths and weaknesses of the model you are currently using? If you don't analyze your model, you will miss the opportunity to emphasize the upsides of your approach and minimize the pitfalls.

energy and go to extremes we'd never have imagined to find their place in a social network of their peers. Sometimes in this search for identity, kids surrender to a common code or set of rules put in place by a peer group. Their status within a specific group depends on how well they maintain the rules for conduct set by the group. To them, this status ranking is directly equivalent to their value as a person. In the case of a kid who's trying to gain status in multiple groups with conflicting rules, this alone can cause huge amounts of stress for him. Even though a parent at home may be telling a kid he is great and precious, if he sees his social ranking as insignificant he cannot reconcile the 2 conflicting messages.

The implications for small groups can vary from week to week. What do we do when our desire in the small group setting is to create an environment where meaningful spiritual journeys begin and are nurtured, but our kids have different agendas? They are obsessed with who they are and how they fit in. This distraction sets the tone for all they think about themselves, and their days may rise and fall on the slightest bit of new information. Every now and then we are on the same page, but often kids and adult leaders seem to have opposing goals. We are trying to build a case for a world perspective based on Christ, while kids are drastically swayed by peer influence. The good news is this: There *are* some strategies we can implement to help them successfully navigate their journey, while still making small group work with and for their friends.

While parents remain the number 1 influencer in the lives of their kids, the kids don't see it that way. There is a natural process of separation from the family as they seek out their own identity. During this period, friends become major players in helping a teen identify who he is in his own eyes—and in the eyes of others. There can be lots of experimentation, preoccupation with self, and a disregard for inconveniencing others. And the fluctuation in their attitudes may become very confusing to adults. A jr. higher might desire the freedom to seek out his identity among his friends, and then quickly shrink back to the security of his family. During this separation from the adult world that once provided their sole stability, kids start to learn more and more from the collective wisdom and direction they get from their peer group. This is exactly why parents should be encouraged to continue talking with their kids even when they don't look or act like they are listening. Parents are still *numero uno,* but peer pressure is a strong 2nd in influencing the choices of early adolescents.

Establish Clear Parameters

If you haven't done so already, you need to make the following decisions:

* if your small group will be open or closed.
* if your group is open to new members coming in at any point during the year, or if kids have to make a commitment to stay with the group for the year.
* if there are only certain nights when they can bring friends to small group, and other nights are only open to the community that has committed to the whole year.

Whichever you decide, you must clearly communicate the parameters to your kids up front so that they will know what to expect and can plan accordingly. Because so many things are changing around them and within them, your kids will appreciate clear boundaries and expectations.

Some small groups are set up in such a way that kids can invite as many friends as they like anytime they wish. These open groups can explode in growth and reproduce themselves during the course of a school year. When you tell kids that small group is a safe place to bring friends to and then you come through on that promise, they begin to trust your word. Your kids will start to feel that small group *is* a safe place to bring their friends, nonbelievers, and friends from other churches. One downside of this approach is that it makes building consistency in relationships more difficult for adult volunteers. A leader may never know who is going to be in his or her group. A small group could end up fluctuating so much that leaders have a difficult time feeling that their time is making an impact on any kids' lives. One major benefit of this approach, however, is that you have the opportunity to involve many more kids in an intimate small group setting. Many churches offer more than 1 type of small group experience. In these situations, once a jr. higher enters the ministry through an open group, after a period of time he is given the option of signing up for a closed group where the commitment is greater.

Regardless of whether you opt for open or closed groups—or a combination of both— the best policy to have concerning friends in a small group setting is to clearly tell kids what to expect and why. Tell them why you have open small groups so they see all the great benefits. Let them know they can bring a friend even if that friend may not come back ever again. They will eventually get the idea and get on board. If you have closed groups, help them see the benefits of meeting with the same group of kids every week and forming stronger bonds. Let kids know that this group is a safe place to say things. That means that everyone in the group must learn to abide by rules such as keeping small group business confidential.

Eagles and Pigeons

Parents want their children to socialize within the context of a safe group. From our own life experiences, we understand the long-term implications that the right or wrong peer group can have on one's life. How do we teach kids in a small group about who Jesus is and how he lived among people, while at the same time shielding them from potentially harmful situations? There has to be some harmony in our message of being like Jesus and reaching out to the hurting, but still practicing good judgment in choosing what crowd to hang with that will encourage spiritual growth.

At a youth leadership event called Student Leadership University, a good friend of mine, Jay Strack, gave an analogy that helps point out the need for kids to find a balance in whom they socialize with. Jay began by having kids look at the life and example of Christ. If Christ were still on this earth in the flesh, he would be hanging with and ministering to the "least of these" (Matthew 25:31-40). We see examples in Christ's life where he touched and spent time with people whom we wouldn't want our own kids to be around—the adulterous woman at the Samaritan well, the demoniac, lepers, ceremonially unclean people, and a whole host of people that we would view as totally inappropriate. How can we teach kids to mimic the life of Christ and then tell them to walk away from his most striking characteristic?

The boundary Jesus drew was very definitive. When moments of crisis arose in his life (such as fatigue from being with the crowds, facing a critical turning point in his ministry, or before he endured the cross), there was a distinct pattern that we should take notice of. In those tough times, Jesus consistently surrounded himself with men who were like-minded. They were people who were about the business of God. They were believers. In Luke 9:58, Jesus issued a warning about the danger in following him, "Foxes have holes and birds of the air have nests, but the Son of Man has no place to lay his head" (*NIV*). He summarized his thoughts on this theme in verse 62, "No one who puts his hand to the plow and looks back is fit for service in the kingdom of God" (*NIV*). These men had put their hands to the plow. Some of them had left promising careers and cushy lifestyles. Because of their desire to be about God's kingdom (even though they didn't understand every aspect of the kingdom Jesus was ushering in) they risked everything. In Jay's words, they were *eagles*, learning to soar.

We also see in Christ an example of loving, working with, ministering to, and rubbing shoulders with *pigeons*. These are people who were in a dark place. They were not his followers, but Jesus spent time with them in order to demonstrate the kingdom of God to them.

At times Jesus drew away from the crowds to be by himself and to seek the Father in prayer and meditation (Mark 1:35; Luke 5:16).

And in Luke 6:12 (just before he chose his 12 disciples), Jesus stole away and prayed all night. After seeking the Father, he surrounded himself with those who could strengthen him in his ministry. If Jesus did so, we need to be bold in challenging kids to be careful in choosing whom they allow to pour into their lives right before critical moments. Quite honestly it was impossible for Jesus to find a spiritual peer. But the men who followed him had enough spiritual presence about them to drop everything in their lives and risk it all to spend 3 years learning from him. They were dedicated and committed to the same work as their Lord.

When tough times came in Christ's life, he surrounded himself with eagles, not pigeons. It was the apostles he asked to stay up and pray with him in the garden the night he knew he would be taken away. The reason is that eagles fly with eagles. The implication for your small group is this: When kids are facing some tough decisions and struggling with various issues, they need to protect themselves by hanging out with the eagles so that they can be well-equipped to follow Jesus' model and minister to the pigeons.

Romance in the Small Group

I met my wife in 7th grade and professed my unfailing love for her to our entire social network. She did not have the same vision for our future. I would have *loved* to be in a small group with her in jr. high, but she would have dreaded the thought. Romance—or the jr. high version of it—is going to happen wherever there are teens. You can choose to fight it, promote it, or downplay it. Whatever your stance, eventually you will have to deal with baggage from jr. high love gone awry. Everybody's favorite loser at life, Charlie Brown, once said, "Nothing takes the taste out of peanut butter quite like unrequited love."[6]

Nothing can bring more awkward silence to the small group than an untimely breakup. The encouraging news is that most likely the previously happy couple had only been "going together" since snack time at the beginning of small group. It wasn't until my sophomore year in college that my wife decided to take me up on my 7th grade marriage proposal! I thank God for the awesome youth coaches who came along my side and helped me concentrate on all-night basketball lock-ins and ski retreats.

Whether we're talking about friends or relationships with the opposite sex, social networks can quickly move and change in the hidden lives of jr. high kids. This is 1 reason why it is so important for leaders to maintain a consistent point of contact and openness in the lives of their small group members.

Redeeming Technology

Because of the electronic revolution, the breakneck speed at which early adolescents socialize has continued to accelerate at an incredible pace (even in the past 3 years). Church youth outings used to be a place where kids could gather in larger numbers to socialize. This was a draw for many youth. Parents, for the most part, seem to feel safe about dropping kids off or endorsing this social gathering more so than dropping younger kids off at the mall or at another parent's house. While kids would be monitored during a church event, there would still be lots of social interaction happening and developing under the watchful eyes of adults nearby.

With online tools such as Facebook and MySpace and mobile applications like text messaging, kids now socialize with any and all friends they choose to without leaving home. They do so while at school (with fingers typing quickly under their desks) and can physically be with their parents while virtually interacting with multiple friends for an entire evening. According to a recent survey at www. symantec.com, kids in the U.S. say they spend 42 hours online each month, while their parents estimate they only spend 18 hours online. American kids also report that that they spend 10 hours a week sending and receiving text messages. In addition, they have an average of 83 online "friends."[7]

Today's teens can categorize social groups in a cleaner fashion with technology. Perhaps they have a group of friends that are church friends. They interact with these friends while keeping a whole other set of friends, conversations, and encounters separate from those church friends. This is simply the world in which they live. Some have tried to detach kids from new technology forms. They might confiscate cell phones from kids during small group time—or even a whole retreat. It is my strong opinion that adults need to be careful not to display harsh attitudes toward these new technologies that kids see as inanimate and neither good nor bad. These technologies have been part of their lives as long as they can remember. A negative attitude toward their use can cause you to lose credibility with kids and drive a wedge in your relationship with them. So move cautiously. In the same way that previous generations fought over rock and roll, many rifts have taken place between adults and kids today over kids' use (or abuse) of technology.

As advanced technology is an indispensable part of who kids are today, you must consider what approach you will take toward its influence on your small group environment. Here's 1 cool way to include texting in the ministry moment. You could ask your kids to get their cell phones out, text someone who's not present, and tell them that they wished they were at small group. Then have them text someone who is *in* the room and tell them they're glad they are there. You could also have kids take notes during small group time and text them to a friend who was not present.

* Are there some creative ways in which you can tap into kids' social networks?
* How can you make texting work for the good of your entire group?
* How connected do you want to be in their lives?
* How does the environment you create lend itself to kids feeling like they are in a safe place?
* Is your small group environment safe enough for kids to invite their friends to? If so, consider that a huge compliment from your kids—and don't take it for granted!

Belonging is the experience we have to offer kids. The community of the church is the place where God has designed for that to happen. The experience of belonging means that you touch others' lives and are touched by theirs. Acts 2:42-47 gives an awesome picture of how this was first played out in the early days of the church:

> They devoted themselves to the apostles' teaching and to the fellowship, to the breaking of bread and to prayer. Everyone was filled with awe, and many wonders and miraculous signs were done by the apostles. All the believers were together and had everything in common. Selling their possessions and goods, they gave to anyone as he had need. Every day they continued to meet together in the temple courts. They broke bread in their homes and ate together with glad and sincere hearts, praising God and enjoying the favor of all the people. And the Lord added to their number daily those who were being saved. (*NIV*)

We are all in this together, sowing seeds, sharing meals, mending wounds, celebrating victories, growing alongside one another in grace and truth. Who wouldn't want to sign up for that?

Do This Now

1. Talk to your kids about why your small group is open or closed. This will help them see a larger purpose for your group than just getting together to hang out.

2. Don't burn a bridge in a relationship when trying to help a teen get some perspective. Acknowledge the depth of how he feels before approaching the issues of why he feels that way.

3. Be careful about how you talk to your group members about their friends. They will remember what you say.

4. Don't downplay the emotion or gravity of any kid's situation. Remember, they are forming their identity. When a jr. higher feels distraught (over something that may seem very trivial to you), validate him. He may not quickly see what is true and what is mere emotion.

5. Don't promote dating or get in on the drama. When asked your opinion, de-escalate the importance of young teen dating, and help them enjoy the fun God has for them in jr. high!

6. What can you do to validate and redeem your teens' use of technology in some creative ways?

Sometimes the Best Wins Are Not in Small Group

As I think back to teachers I had over the years and try to pinpoint exact lessons that they taught me, a few memories stand out. I remember Sandy Christian helping her class make clay topographical maps of the Promised Land. I recall the smell more than anything. I also remember Uncle Larry teaching us about Hell. He said that my brother's watch would melt there. That made an impression on me! Oh, and one time my youth pastor Troy faked an argument with his wife Jodi about losing the car keys. It was dramatic . . . but I don't remember what the lesson was about.

What kind of impressions are you making in the lives of the jr. high kids you have been called to love, serve, and challenge to a deeper walk with Christ? If your most committed, spiritually hungry teens come to church (not just the small group meeting) 3 hours a week, 12 hours a month, that adds up to a total of 18 full days of hanging at church during a 3-year jr. high tenure. How big of an impact can you have on them during that time period? That is why it is so key to get involved in their lives outside the church building. We can't expect all life transformation to take place while kids are in our world—we must take the bold step to engage them in theirs!

Great Strides

Old cowboys say that horses are usually born early in the night as a built-in defense mechanism. Many predators attack in the morning, and by that time it is believed that a young colt can already run up to 80 percent of its life's top speed. It's amazing that after just a few hours of life a young colt can be up and running so fast! He may only be a few hours old, but he can accelerate.

The same can be true for jr. high kids. Though young in their faith, in a very short time they have the ability to make huge strides in understanding and living out their faith. Often when a jr. higher makes a huge change in his spiritual walk, it is the result of an encounter that has occurred outside the regular small group meeting. The most unlikely of kids can take great strides, and that is an exciting aspect about working with jr. high teens. Much like the newborn colt galloping at astonishing speeds, it can be the 1 kid who seems like he has the farthest distance to go who abruptly takes great strides.

Typically, when this kind of spiritual leap takes place in a teen's life, an adult has gone the extra mile with him, and BAM—it just happens. An adult may have spent the 1 night she had open that week driving to another town to see a young woman run in a cross-country race for 20 seconds. Thirty minutes in the car each way, another fast-food meal—and all for 20 seconds. But those final seconds made all the difference. We can talk all we want about desiring relationship, and we can invite with words, but the extra investment resonates deep within the teen, assuring her that the mentorship we offer is sincere.

On a cognitive level, kids naturally compartmentalize their lives for survival. It's not that they don't see a bigger picture of how things fit together, it's just easier to process everything about a certain situation or place they find themselves in when they erect walls and can keep complex things separated. They have complexities in their home lives, school lives, friends' lives, extracurricular lives, and church lives that they are trying to figure out. And when something complex from 1 particular situation bleeds over into another area of their lives, it may take them awhile to adjust. For younger jr. highers, the first reaction to seeing an adult leader at a cross-country meet may not be one of excitement. It might be shocking to them—they simply aren't used to thinking of life holistically. And when you show up to visit them at a soccer game, it explodes the little church box your relationship used to be limited to. They now see you and the possibilities for your relationship in a whole new light. Simply talking about how deep we want our relationships to grow doesn't yield the same result. We must validate the authenticity of small group outside the walls of the group meeting.

Belonging

We have larger goals in mind for our kids than a sense of belonging. But all other things we want to accomplish flow naturally

So You're a Volunteer

Hanging out with kids in a variety of settings is perhaps more important than anything you will ever teach in small group. But there are a few ground rules you should follow:

* Never be alone with a kid. If the meeting is in your home, and none of your other family members are around, ask another volunteer to stay with you until parents pick up the last teen.
* If kids start talking about their parents in a negative light, try not to agree (even if what they are saying is true!). You never know what a kid will repeat to his parents. Instead of being negative, go overboard to try to help kids see some things from their parents' perspective.
* Watch your tone of voice, body language, and underlying attitude when talking about other adults with whom kids interact (such as coaches and teachers). As an ambassador for Christ, your speech and attitude should always be above reproach.
* If you have a mixed-gender group, when you are discussing sensitive topics like sex, recruit a volunteer from the opposite sex to help you. Find someone who complements your gift mix.

from it. The small group is the platform for recognizing how lives are intertwined through rich, shared, deeply growing relationships. A sense of belonging starts to develop when we value kids as individuals and not just as attendees of the church function we lead.

If we can get our kids to feel a deep sense of belonging through realizing that they contribute something of value to the group, then the foundation has been laid for all kinds of great things. How do we get them to realize that they are extremely valuable to the group? What about when we *don't* believe that a particular teen brings something special to the table? The answers to both of these questions often are revealed when we get involved in teens' lives outside the small group meeting.

On Foreign Soil

So you've decided to take a shot and launch out into uncharted territory. You are willing to hang out with kids on their turf. That is awesome because there are many great opportunities to build bridges of trust and respect with kids when you venture out into their world. Here are some travel tips for your trek into "no man's land":

* Since this is *their* turf, remember you do not make the rules and call all the shots. Some adult leaders never go and meet kids on their turf for this reason.
* Kids must feel your confidence. You didn't just *happen* to show up; you did it on purpose. Don't trivialize your attempt to meet them and invest in them. At the same time, don't drone on about how awesome you are for showing up. If given the chance, recognize that the event is important to you, too, and you're glad you had the opportunity to connect outside of the small-group environment.

- You may want to show up near the middle of the game or event so that you'll have time to stay after and connect with the teen. Kids won't count the hours, but they will count the quality connection.
- Be bold, but be cautious. If the opportunity presents itself, interact with the teen after his activity. Be careful not to overplay your relationship in front of his friends. He may be nervous about how you will come off to them (remember, you are bringing together 2 distinct parts of his life, and he may be uncomfortable with this).
- Gain respect by showing respect. If you are not sure what is safe in the relationship and don't want to push her into freak-out mode, ask ahead of time, "Do you have time to talk after your game?" This gives her an out, and you have communicated respect.
- Remember this is not the time to teach. Ecclesiastes 3:1 says, "For everything there is a season, a time for every activity under heaven." This is not the time for you to wear the teacher hat.
- Don't try to be someone else—be you! Kids will see through any attempt to take on a different persona.
- Pray before you go. It is a spiritual win.
- Encourage the teen you are going to see. This is not rocket science; it should be obvious, but people forget to do it all the time.
- Don't do anything that might show up a parent. Never burn a bridge with parents to build a bridge with their kid. The payoff isn't worth it.
- Don't take yourself too seriously. Be goofy if you need to. Some people have the gift of disarming kids immediately. They are usually people who don't try to put up a front.
- Watch your witness. Your life is always being observed.
- Don't be upset if one day outside the church a kid desires relationship and the next day he ignores you. He may be struggling with autonomy from the familial unit and anything that might be associated with that—which could include you.

✦ Think like Jesus. He spent time in the temple among the rabbis and teachers of the law, but he also got out with the people. He met them on their turf. He ate with them, listened to them, met their families, and touched them on a deeper level.

Winning Together

The church has attempted to have age-appropriate programming for kids, and with good reason. But if it is not careful, the church's approach can result in too many silos. In most churches, families are split up generationally as soon as they walk in the door. The small group can do much to help strengthen family ties. If parents are informed about what is going on in small group and are invited to participate from time to time (through providing snacks, driving to events, or attending a special night), and if adult leaders spend some time on kids' turf, the small group ministry can have a positive effect on the family unit. Parents are *not* the enemy—we are on the same team. We must do all that we can to partner together in helping jr. high teens achieve their potential.

Any positive interaction adults have with kids outside the normal functions of small group will broaden the perspective that kids have of the church, its people, and its possible

So You're in a Small Church

A great way to get kids talking is to ask them to give you an overview of their upcoming week. Write down opportunities where you can make a connection outside of small group. You may be involved in more than 1 ministry in your church, so don't burn yourself out trying to attend all your kids' activities. Do what you can. You are not going to be able to attend every game of every kid in your small group. At the same time, don't let that stop you from attending the one(s) that you can!

Once you arrive at a teen's event, don't embarrass them! It's one thing to make a big deal about them so they know you appreciate them, but it is another to go overboard and embarrass them in front of their friends. Kids will test you to see how true and legit your love is for them. Be prepared to pass more than 1 test before they let you into their lives.

impact upon their lives. Kids, like adults, hit lulls and roadblocks in their spiritual journeys. If small group encounters have become stagnant for a teen, his attitude can take a different turn due to some extra initiative from a leader. Defining moments can carry us all through what could be very lonely times. Some of these defining moments can happen for kids when something beyond the normal happens—when an adult does something unexpected in their lives. It could be as simple as talking about life while eating ice cream at Dairy Queen after school. A little extra special attention never hurt anybody and an intentional investment in a teen rarely goes unnoticed. ✦

Do This Now

1. Do a periodic audit for each kid in your small group. Many times we think about where the whole group is or we gravitate towards those whom we naturally click with. Take a moment to think intentionally about where every kid is spiritually and what could take them to the next level.

2. Conduct an audit of your meeting space. Is your small group environment conducive to kids opening up? Analyze what setup changes could make a huge difference in your small group.

3. Double up! Make an event out of someone's activity. Invite other kids from the small group to meet you at (or go with you to) another kid's event.

4. Don't make it a debt/debtor relationship. Attend a special function because you care. Don't leverage it in an unhealthy way to commit kids to something else.

5. Don't judge the success of your ventures into kids' worlds by the facial expression, demeanor, or actions of the kid you went to see. There can be many reasons he might ignore you outside the safe confines of the small group bubble. Be assured that the impression your effort left is far greater than what you can see.

Build a Fire and Dance Around It

Recently my wife and I spent some time with a couple who mentor us as parents. Their 2 children are older than ours. One is in high school and the other in jr. high. During our visit with them, both children pointed out, in casual conversation, numerous experiences that had made an impact on them. Without prompting the conversation toward the topic of faith traditions, the kids brought up significant rites-of-passage events from their lives. They commented on the change in their status and what it had meant to them. One example was the few years of anticipation they had gone through before they could see the movie, *The Passion of the Christ*. They had not been allowed to see this movie until their parents felt like they were mature enough in their faith and life experience to handle the content. It had been 6 months since both kids had seen the movie. Indeed, it had made a profound impact on them.

Are you on the lookout for mile markers on the side of the road that you can anticipate and experience with kids in such a way that the whole road trip is about God? There are many mile markers that point to God, but if we are not carefully setting them up and helping kids process them in the light of spiritual things, they become insignificant, and eventually we forget the real reason we are on the road trip. When we intentionally make memories centered around our faith, we build a foundation for our kids that will deepen their character and help them swim against the popular current. If the moments we celebrate the most are of this world, then we are promoting an identity formed around today's culture, not around Christ.

Look into Kids' Lives

The process of walking with kids and making faith memories with them happens within the larger context of mentoring. Mentoring is a hot concept in the world of business. The word is used to describe what takes place in a variety of settings—whether through an apprenticeship, professional coaching and counseling, or on-the-job training. A mentor is someone who has been down the road (in a career or in life) that the one being mentored will travel. The task of looking into the lives of the kids you have been called to mentor takes time. It happens when you hang out with them. It happens when you attend their ball games, plays, and concerts. It happens when you listen to them talk about how they perceive the world around them.

As I read the Gospels, I can't help but get caught up in the pictures of Jesus walking, eating, and going through ordinary, everyday tasks with his disciples. My imagination, and even my theology, wonders what inside jokes they had. Which disciple had to always get the firewood? Who did Jesus give a hard time for having stinky feet? (Couldn't he just heal them?) If you've never thought about Jesus

So You Get Paid

How do you emulate for your leaders the type of mentoring you desire for them to have with kids? Here are some practical ideas:

* Every now and then, show kids that you care more about them than you care about your agenda. Be willing to scrap the study and ask them to talk about their activities outside of church. Then, as appropriate, affirm their areas of giftedness.
* Pair up younger volunteers with a parent who may not connect with kids as easily. Allow the parent to take care of details such as arranging rides, baking snacks, and communicating with parents of new kids to the group. As these details are taken care of, younger volunteers will be able to focus more on the task of mentoring.
* Consider using different curriculum for different small groups. Your older, core kids might need something deeper than some of the other groups. And it is OK if a 6th grade boys small group's main attraction is playing basketball, if that will help them develop deeper relationships with adults.

Ask yourself:

* How can you bring God into the context of rites-of-passage events your kids are already involved in outside the church?
* How are you equipping parents and volunteers to plan and pull off significant rites-of-passage events?

This could be your
niche! Let's face it,
pulling off a rites-
of-passage event as
was described in this
chapter can be a ton
of work. Can you cook
the food, make the slide
and video presentation,
buy or make the tokens,
do publicity, and bug
people until they think
it's important, too? Is
God calling and equip-
ping you to be the
champion and vision-
caster in your church
for events like this?
God may be dealing
with you in an Exodus
31-type of moment
right now.

passing gas around the campfire (6th grade
boys love thinking about this), how can you
believe he was fully human and fully God?
The journey we see Jesus on with his disciples
is the very journey we are called to imitate
with our kids.

As you journey with jr. highers, you perceive
the unique talents and gifts that God gave
them (James 1:17)—gifts they often do not yet
realize they have. Many kids would never see
these things on their own. They lack the life
experience and objectivity. We know some
things about them better than they can grasp
themselves. We can see things hidden in them
that need developing, even when they don't
believe in themselves or in us. These developing young adults have raw material that can
be shaped into qualities that God's larger
community desperately needs. The health and
longevity of our local churches depends on the
contributions that our kids bring. As we pass
on God's truths to the next generation, the larger community of the
church is refreshed in many ways.

We need to pray intentionally that God would reveal kids' giftedness to us. Sometimes we are afraid to talk to them about their individual areas of giftedness because we have no clue what God is doing
in their lives. Sometimes we only see a socially awkward mess every
time they begin to talk. It is clear that they are asking huge questions
about what they have to offer. Some kids slip through the cracks
because the church never answered the most pressing questions in
their lives. We need to affirm their questions even if we don't know

the answers immediately. They should know that they won't find the answers on their own; we must let them know that we are interceding on their behalf, asking God to reveal his will for their lives.

Celebrate Their Unique Gifts

We need to tell jr. highers that they are special and that God has put something inside them that the whole group needs. Exodus 31 exemplifies this truth. After God brought the children of Israel out of Egypt, they camped at the foot of Mount Sinai. After 400 years of captivity they were free. Unfortunately they were a people without an identity. They had no culture of their own. After all that time in captivity, they had grown familiar with the festivals and traditions of the Egyptians. God had delivered them from that bondage, escaping all that they had known. God was calling them to be a great nation, and he knew exactly what that would take. But surely they wondered how that would take place. How were these former slaves to become a great nation that all other nations would fear? While Moses was up on the mountain receiving detailed plans, God was moving at the foot of the mountain within the camp.

> Then the LORD said to Moses, "Look, I have specifically chosen Bezalel son of Uri, grandson of Hur, of the tribe of Judah. I have filled him with the Spirit of God, giving him great wisdom, ability, and expertise in all kinds of crafts. He is a master craftsman, expert in working with gold, silver, and bronze. He is skilled in engraving and mounting gemstones and in carving wood. He is a master at every craft!
> "And I have personally appointed Oholiab son of Ahisamach, of the tribe of Dan, to be his assistant.

Moreover, I have given special skill to all the gifted craftsmen so they can make all the things I have commanded
you to make: the Tabernacle; the Ark of the Covenant;
the Ark's cover—the place of atonement; all the furnish-
ings of the Tabernacle; the table and its utensils; the
pure gold lampstand with all its accessories; the incense
altar; the altar of burnt offering with all its utensils;
the washbasin with its stand; the beautifully stitched
garments—the sacred garments for Aaron the priest,
and the garments for his sons to wear as they minister
as priests; the anointing oil; the fragrant incense for the
Holy Place. The craftsmen must make everything as I
have commanded you" (Exodus 31:1-11).

In what ways do you see God gifting the kids in your small group
with expertise in various crafts? How have you seen him filling them
with his Spirit? Which ones has he endowed with intelligence and
wisdom beyond their years? If you have seen God's gifts in their
lives, affirm their giftedness and celebrate!

Join in What God Is Doing

It is not in God's nature to call us to a job and then not equip us.
His *better* is better than ours. Sometimes he is doing something that
we seem to be fighting against. When Jesus foretold his death on the
cross, the apostles fought against it. They saw the end of a revolution.
God saw the last sacrifice. They only saw the cross, while his eyes
were on the empty tomb. It happens with your small group, too. You
may only see chaos, but God is building and nurturing behind the
scenes. You may only see your kids' uncontrolled self-expression, but
God sees giftedness from the Holy Spirit.

How can you see more clearly from God's point of view? What is he preparing in the seemingly messy lives of jr. high kids that you need to affirm? Chances are that God is in the process of gifting your kids to fill some holes for the benefit of the entire church. Rarely are God's gifts just about us as individuals—they come with a blessing to the whole community. You have the awesome honor of helping to usher in God's new gifts to the entire church.

You've Got Something to Say

Once you've looked into kids' lives and have seen their gifts, you have to earn the right to share. It is a privilege to prophetically speak into the life of a young person, and it's one that you should not take lightly. Keep in mind that this can take some time. Frustration comes about when the gift of speaking into teens' lives is taken for granted. Small group time can be met with blank faces, and the leader's expectations are not realized. You may need to recognize where the real starting point is in the relationship-building process. There are many things that could be viewed as progress on this road that could easily be overlooked and not celebrated by the small group community. The neglect and dismissal of these wins communicates to the group that the relational foundation isn't necessary. Anything that builds on this most important foundation should be brought to the attention of the entire group and affirmed.

Reclaim the *Brother Bear* Model

Jr. high small groups are ministries of transition. One of the greatest lessons for transition into tween ministry within the church came from the Disney movie *Brother Bear*. In the movie a group of boys are walked through the transition from boyhood to adulthood with the help of spiritual mentors. The movie clearly illustrated the collective responsibility of a community for helping adolescents through a very important rite of passage—or milestone—on the road to adulthood.

A rite of passage is a ritual or ceremony signifying an event in a person's life that is indicative of a transition from one stage to another, as from adolescence to adulthood. No jr. high kid is going to define a special moment this way. To him it is simply a defining moment when he feels hope, direction, and support—and a real sense that he is going to make it through this "growing up thing" in a way that makes him proud. These moments happen in the life of every adolescent.

Our job is to help kids see God's presence in their own journey. When the adult community fails to celebrate these rites of passage, kids will find their own methods and mile markers to celebrate within their own private community. This is a very scary thing. Inevitably their new methods for signifying mile markers on their journey will not be centered on God. The more opportunities we miss to set the table within the context of the church, the greater significance kids' own rites-of-passage ceremonies have. At risk is our influence on kids for the rest of their lives.

What events get more hype? What activities get more of our time and money? Is it the next big movie blockbuster, or is it the first time kids participate in communion? Is it our teens' first car, or is it their baptism? Is a sports banquet at school anticipated and celebrated in a more meaningful way than a rites-of-passage ceremony event at church? Can small groups even compete in this arena?

Rites of passage are a strong force in so many cultures around the world. To our shame, we have neglected this powerful shaping experience in too many of our faith traditions in America. In the movie *Brother Bear*, a young Native American boy was given a token—a wooden bear on a necklace that he was to wear. He was told that the souvenir bear pointed to his special ability—rough as it might yet be—to love people. He didn't see this trait in himself. He doubted the truth and even came to resent the gesture. Regardless, the adults in his life saw something in him that he would grow into more fully. They saw beneath his exterior and opened his eyes to the possibility his life could become. This symbol became for him a tactile reminder of the specific call on his life—to love people.

The boy received his special token in the presence of the whole community, and a party ensued around the campfire. How awesome would it be if we constantly sat down our jr. highers and affirmed the gifts that we see in them? We need to let them know that those gifts are needed in the body of Christ—both now and when they graduate from high school.

In *Brother Bear*, the rules for the journey were clearly understood by the leaders and current participants, and they were modeled for younger children to aspire to. The community walked their young through a process of maturing into adulthood. The involvement of the total community was the key to success. There was great significance in the rite of passage they had set up. The youth were allowed to put their hand on the wall and join the larger adult community while the whole community gathered around them and acknowledged their growth. They made it a *big stinking* deal.

Perhaps the best place to start in remedying the situation would be for the senior pastor to conduct a rites of passage experience in "big church." Make this really important. Let's build a fire, dance in big church, and hand out wooden tokens to our kids.

A Rites of Passage Roadmap

If you decide to make a big deal of a rites-of-passage ceremony for jr. high kids (and I hope you will), here are some helpful tips for your planning:

* The ceremony must include a significant change in status that is affirmed by the larger community in a "big church" setting. Perhaps have 2 separate events, 1 in which the "men" are welcomed into the village, and another where the "women" take their place among the other females of the community.

* There needs to be a public acknowledgment of growth and achievement that truly merits the change in status. What must they do to be affirmed as adults?

* Commemorate the experience with something tactile: build something, give them a token. Kind words from the senior pastor don't complete the experience alone. Hang something around their necks and give them some sort of special gift.

* Imitate what happens at a rite-of-passage sports banquet:
  * Have them dress up and invite their parents to attend.
  * Serve them a nice meal.
  * Show slides depicting the struggles and victories the group has experienced together.
  * Call kids up 1 by 1, and have adult leaders tell fun stories about some ways in which they have grown up.
  * Celebrate and cry together.
  * Give them something to take home: a letter, a book, a piece of jewelry.

What is the most significant impact you can make in the kingdom of God? Introducing others to Jesus Christ and helping to transform their lives through the power of the Holy Spirit. Yes, it's time-consuming, but, man, is it ever worth it! Belonging is a great gift to have within your power to give. You are not alone—and neither are your kids. The Holy Spirit ministers alongside you. As a leader you play a key, God-appointed role in this transformation process. You can do this, you can enjoy it, and you can make a significant impact in the lives of jr. highers . . . without turning into a bear. ✦

Do This Now

1. Rent *Brother Bear* and watch it.

2. Jr. high kids get excited about what you promote as good. Think about what milestones you should be elevating.

3. If you haven't been to one lately, attend a sports banquet for one of your kids, and take good notes.

4. After you celebrate a rite of passage, paint a picture for the next step in the process. Don't leave kids hanging. They will have a renewed sense of energy, so meet that with fresh direction.

10

You Can Do This . . . and You Should

I'd like to ask you to take a journey with me. No, we're not going to Hawaii, though that does sound like an awesome idea! You don't have to physically go anywhere in order to go on this trip. And you won't have any jr. highers with you. Cool? Go get your cozy slippers, and we'll start. I'll wait. Got 'em? The cozy slippers, I mean? OK, sit back and get comfortable. I mean . . . hold on! It might be a bumpy ride.

Now picture yourself back in jr. high. Remember the sights, sounds, and smells (like old food under your bed) of your room. Remember your favorite shirt, your favorite class in school—if you had one. Who were some of your best friends? What happened during your best summer during your jr. high years? Do you have a most embarrassing moment? Take your time; I'll wait.

Now I'd like you to think of the person who had the single most impact on your faith during that time. Perhaps no one did, and your faith journey didn't start until later. What might it have been like if a spiritual encounter had come sooner? What happened in jr. high that prepared your heart for that encounter to come later? If an encounter with someone who deepened your faith *did* happen in jr. high, what was that person like? How did you meet him or her (assuming it wasn't a parent)? When did you start to trust this person?

What friends came along during that important time in your life and shared your experience? What were the defining moments in that relationship with an adult? How did that relationship with the significant adult end, or is it still going on? If you had the opportunity to tell them something today about the impact they made on your life during those years, what would you say to them? Did that encounter play into your desire to work with kids now? What lessons did you catch from them that you fall back on today in working with jr. high kids?

Feel free to go get a cup of coffee before we continue the next leg of our journey. I'll wait. Got it? OK. Now I'd like you to think about

Do the following:

* Conduct a motivation audit. Are you in a dangerous place because of your current motivation? Ask yourself honestly, "Why am I doing what I am doing in ministry?" Is it about bringing glory to you or to God? How does this affect your decisions and philosophy for working with kids?

* Join a community of other jr. high leaders to find encouragement and a safe place to vent.

* Use Facebook, blogs, and youth leader training seminars to connect with others who share your awesome calling. Don't live on an island! Other people undoubtedly feel just as you do. You may very well be their source of encouragement today!

a specific kid in your small group. What kinds of challenges is he (or she) going through? What's his home life like? Now imagine that teen as a freshman in high school. Picture him at a school activity that he enjoys. Picture him getting his driver's license, going to the prom, and then celebrating his high school graduation with his family. Imagine him going to college, being dropped off away from home as a freshman. Picture him finding his future mate and getting married—then seeing his firstborn child for the first time.

OK, you can come back to Earth now. What strong impressions struck you as you thought about your jr. high years? What future visions did you get for the jr. higher whose life you are involved in? It's exciting to know that we can help shape the people that our kids will eventually become. Fruit will come from the seeds you are currently sowing. The investment you are making now can have a rippling effect on many people way into the future. Your obedience to God in telling the next generation of his praiseworthy deeds will touch more lives than God may ever reveal to you while you're on this earth. That's pretty heavy duty, huh?

Adults Worth Following

Our culture today holds up talented individuals on the screen, stage, and in sports arenas that teens often adore. As adults, we are quicker to see through the outer facades than kids are. But before we judge our kids too harshly, we should admit that in reality, we too have our own grown-up versions of people we aspire to become.

Some of the most effective jr. high workers I know are not the sort of people that kids flock to and ask for autographs. You might see them and not immediately peg them as people whom kids want to idolize, seek out, or hang out with. Yet because they are obedient to their calling, they invest in lives and bear fruit. There is something charmingly disarming about an imperfect adult who makes a huge impact on kids' lives. Does that describe you?

Do you sense that you have a heavenly calling to dedicate a portion of your life to helping kids do life? Do you feel that you are to contend for the hearts and minds and souls of today's youth against the forces of evil in this world (Ephesians 6:12)? Whether you're considering working with jr. highers or you're already doing it, I hope there is a healthy sense of awe at the weight of it all. You've been called to be more than just a warm body in a meeting room. You've been called to make a real difference in kids' lives. God is looking for people who have earnestly thought out their calling. And if God has called you into this, be assured that he will give you the skills you need to accomplish the task! Nothing escapes the watchful eye of our Father in Heaven who cares for all his children.

Don't Rob God

The apostle Paul spent a great deal of time in 1 Corinthians 12 explaining that the church is the body of Christ and we are all individual members of his body, each with varying gifts. All parts are needed in the body, but each part must do its specific job or the body won't function at peak performance. Think about it this way: When you are not serving in the right place, you are robbing God. If you have never done so, I encourage you to be still before God, and listen to him with a serious intent on hearing his designs for how you should serve. If you are *not* called to work with jr. high kids, but you drudge through it anyway, then you are robbing God *twice.*

The dispenser of talents has gifted you for something the church needs. When we discover those gifts and the Holy Spirit confirms it through other people's comments, the fruit we see, and our creative abilities in that area, we should work at it with all our hearts as working for the Lord and not for men (Colossians 3:23, *NIV*). If that is *not* mentoring jr. high kids, then we are robbing God in the first place by not serving in the area he intended us to serve. Secondly, we could be hindering the growth of other people by not being obedient to our calling. Perhaps God has made someone for the job we might be toiling in right now and they can't serve as long as we are taking up their space.

God's kingdom will advance with or without my help or yours. But when we are not serving in the right place, it not only touches our lives but so many other people around us. Seeking out our areas of giftedness through prayer and earnest listening to the Holy Spirit is a very serious thing, and the community of believers should be a part of that process. This is exactly the same process we are trying to pass on to our teens.

You Are Not Alone

I had my own plans for ministry. God let me realize some of them, but I would never have guessed the direction he chose to take me. Proverbs 3:5, 6 challenged me to, "Trust in the LORD with all your heart; do not depend on your own understanding. Seek his will in all you do, and he will show you which path to take." God not only knew how to direct my paths, but he also knew what would be best for my family and for the kingdom, and he knew how to prepare me for it! God also knew how to increase my joy in the midst of the process. God knows how to prepare us for works. We just need to be obedient to the tasks at hand.

People who have discerned that their calling *is* to work with jr. high kids are a band of battle-hardened warriors who will gladly welcome you to the ranks. But they will also be the first to tell you that it is difficult. The rewards are great but can take many years in coming. We might even have to be willing to wait until Heaven to see all the fruit we've helped produce. In short, ministry costs. King David understood that any offering to God that takes its toll on us—whether time, worried nights, disappointment, sadness, uncomfortable cots to sleep on, or lots of pizza money—is an offering acceptable to God. David said, "I will not present burnt offerings to the LORD my God that have cost me nothing" (2 Samuel 24:24).

Often when youth leaders want to quit, or question their effectiveness, they talk about the results that they can see. But there is an element of trusting God and his Holy Spirit for the things we cannot

So You're a Volunteer

When I encounter youth workers who are discouraged, crushed, and freaking out, I usually discover that their motivation has dangerously shifted. This shift has occurred slowly over time, unnoticeable even to them until they slow down to think it out. When our motivation is for people, we are aligned with God's heart. When our motivation is to lift up Jesus, we are aligned with God the Father. One simple test is to ask yourself periodically if what you are doing will bring glory to God or to yourself. The lines can quickly get blurred. If the primary reason you are working with kids is so that you can be close to your own kids and their friends, you will quickly find yourself on a slippery slope. Any other starting point for motivation—no matter how just it may sound on its own—will fail if Christ is not at the core of your reasoning for ministry. We can't heal our past through ministry, we can't fix our own future by working with kids, and we can't make up for something we feel guilty for. All of these starting points will leave us empty.

see. If we are listening to the Holy Spirit's direction as we invest in the lives of jr. highers, we must trust that God is working behind the scenes in some powerful ways. The answers, wisdom, and tools needed to set kids on their way rarely lie within you. Rather, they come through the power of the Holy Spirit working in all those who are obedient to him.

To walk alongside kids at this time is a great honor I hope you will never forget. Inside every one of these precious kids you spend time with already lies the adults they will become. They are in the critical season that shapes so much of who they will be. Crisis points in our lives always carry the greatest potential to cultivate deep roots. While the whole world might seem like it is falling apart to a kid, the conditions may actually be ripe to plant and cultivate a deeply-rooted faith.

So You're in a Small Church

One thing that you have in common with larger youth ministries is this: You should do everything you can to help create a safe place for your kids. If you live in a community in which the same families have lived there for perhaps generations, you may be tempted to skip the following guideline, but I strongly encourage you to implement it. Have everyone who wants to work with teens in your church fill out a background check form and disclosure statement claiming any previous felony or convictions that could prohibit them from working with kids. Also have all adults sign commitment forms to follow church rules that specify how you will handle discipline problems. It might be awkward having some people go through this protocol to work with kids, but if everyone has to comply—even the senior pastor—it won't feel so awkward. Your kids can never be too safe, and you will be served well by giving due diligence to these matters.

At the end of the day, concentrate on the main thing, which is building relationships with kids! If you're in a small church, you might be freed up from many distractions to ministry that can plague larger churches—things like the proper way to check kids into Wednesday night programming and traffic flow problems. The kids God has called you to walk with are most likely not bothered that your whole youth group *is* a small group. More than anything you ever teach them, they will remember the kind of relationship you built with them.

You may feel that your jr. high kids are the most unappreciated, neglected, and shrugged-off group of people in the church. Join the crowd. You may get the high school hand-me-downs and that sweet youth room with no windows in the church basement. At times you feel that you are the lone survivor on an island—and even now you see the shark-infested waters all around you. You see the great potential for jr. high ministry in your church, yet you have to move mountains just to get an announcement in "big church." Don't despair. There is encouragement in knowing that you are not alone. When you bravely put your hand to the plow of jr. high youth ministry, you join with an elite group of many other like-minded crazies.

My friend Rick Bundschuh is a former jr. high worker turned senior pastor at a church in Kauai, Hawaii. Tough gig, I know. Rick took the job just so he could make the jr. high ministry the biggest line item in the whole church budget—and that is what he did! I've heard Rick say that the last budget he would ever cut in his church would be for the jr. high. While you may not be blessed to have a senior pastor who gets jr. high ministry like Rick does, take confidence in the fact that there are other people out there who are as nuts about jr. high ministry as you are. (By the way, if you are going to ask for the largest budget line next year at your church, please record that meeting and post it on YouTube® for the rest of us. Just keep the cameras on the faces of your church leadership!)

You Are Important

Kids need more than 1 positive adult role model in their lives. If there is already someone who seems to be actively involved with the jr. high kids at your church, don't assume that you are not needed! You serve an important role. I can think of several adults who played significantly different roles during my jr. high years, and they were all influential. Offer what you can. The impact you make may not always be equivalent to the investment made!

Jr. High Leaders Rock

Steve was involved in my life for 2 weeks during the summer of my 8th grade year. He was awesome! He played guitar very well, had really cool rock 'n roll hair, and invested in me even though his window of time was small. I painted alongside him on a mission trip for 1 week and then we were both at a camp the following week. The relationship meant the world to me. Based on a few lunches and a few gallons of paint, what I perceived his walk with Jesus to be became a lifelong image of the Christian walk for me. Steve was the coolest youth worker I had in jr. high, but there were many others who played various roles and helped shape my young adolescent years.

Because kids have a variety of personalities, they resonate with different adults. They also need different personalities in different situations in their lives. Steve was there and gone, but there were other adults in my life that spent countless hours with me, like Bill and Connie. My wife and I still see Bill and Connie when we visit our home church. The most memorable event Bill ever pulled off was a dramatic impersonation of Elvis Presley that he seemed to enjoy way too much. (We turned the basement lights off and turned on the American DJ® disco ball!)

I don't remember the theological point behind Bill's sideburn lecture, but the pizza served at their house every Sunday night was the highlight of my week. We didn't watch TV or play video games. There was no draw to get us all there, but a group of about 6 of us rarely missed those evenings in their living room. Bill and Connie had so much they were juggling in their own lives. If anyone in our church didn't have time to be jr. high small group leaders it was legitimately them. But by investing in me during those jr. high years, they poured their lives into my marriage, my kids, and everything my life will touch from here to eternity.

You are important! Some of what you do may seem insignificant to you. It's just pizza and an hour or so after church, right? Remember, God takes that which may seem insignificant and uses it to draw kids to himself.

You Can Do This

My prayer for you is that you will receive a new sense of ability in your role as a jr. high worker, not because of the knowledge that is in your head, but because of the Holy Spirit that dwells within you. This is big business you are called to. It is such big business that it is at the top of God's agenda. God desires for all people to come to him. Second Peter 3:9 says, "The Lord is not slow in keeping his promise, as some understand slowness. He is patient with you, not wanting anyone to perish, but everyone to come to repentance" (*NIV*).

Jr. high kids are at an age that research shows is the most receptive time within the human experience that people come to follow Jesus. One survey that really helped to raise the banner for effective jr. high ministry came from George Barna in his book, *Transforming Children into Spiritual Champions*. He said this:

A series of studies we conducted regarding the age at which people accept Christ as their Savior highlights the importance of having people invite Jesus into their heart as their Savior when they are young. We discovered that the probability of someone embracing Jesus as his or her Savior was 32 percent for those between the ages of 5 and 12; and 6 percent for people 19 or older. In other words, if people do not embrace Jesus Christ as their Savior before they reach their teenage years, the chance of their doing so at all is slim.[8]

If this were the only reason one could find for desiring to be a jr. high youth worker, it would be a very good one. If you are doing the work of God and he wants to you to bear fruit, then he will give you the tools you need to succeed. It's not up to you and your abilities. It is up to him. The apostle John promised, "The one who is in you is greater than the one who is in the world" (1 John 4:4, *NIV*).

Excuses

If by seeking God and listening to others you have discerned you are called to work with jr. high kids, but you still have some questions in respect to your perceived lack of ability, what should you do? Here are a few common feelings among your comrades-in-arms:

✸ I Can't Teach

During the jr. high years, kids are at their peak mental preparedness for storing, memorizing, and categorizing raw information. For years kids have been fed content, and now for the first time they are wondering how it all fits together. While it's true that some leaders are more gifted than others in the area of teaching (Ephesians 4:11), the jr. high years are not the time for lectures only. This is when the wise teacher listens more than he talks. You can do this! God appoints special people to tasks that he has especially gifted them to perform (Ephesians 4:12). He has given some to be jr. high small group leaders.

✻ I'm Not Smart Enough

One of the greatest fears that inhibits potentially great jr. high small group leaders is the fear of not knowing all the answers to questions jr. highers might ask. I've never had a kid look at me like I was a moron for saying, "I don't know, can I get back to you later on that one?" They look at me like I'm a moron for lots of other reasons, but not for that one. Generally, it is well received by kids when we tell them we honestly don't know.

Why are we so afraid of not knowing the answer? I love the words of the apostle Paul in 1 Corinthians 1. I can appreciate a man of sarcasm and that is exactly where Paul begins in verse 20. He essentially asks God, "So who is this wise person that knows it all anyway?" The answer: God, the one that lives in us, made all wisdom known and unknown to man. Since God's power lives in me if I am walking with him, I trust that he will reveal to me all the wisdom I need to lead a jr. high small group. I actually laugh out loud when I read verses 26 and 27 with jr. high youth leaders: "Remember, dear brothers and sisters, that few of you were wise in the world's eyes or powerful or wealthy when God called you. Instead, God chose things the world considers foolish in order to shame those who think they are wise. And he chose things that are powerless to shame those who are powerful."

There you have it. You can be really smart—or really foolish—and God can still use you powerfully in jr. high ministry. He wants you to realize that it's not about your mad skills, but his, so that you will not boast about yourself, but will "boast in the Lord" (v. 31, *NIV*). All the darts the enemy throws your way to get you off track can be deflected, not because of who you are, but because of who God is. He has all the answers you'll ever need.

Trust and Obey

It comes down to obedience and trust. A hymn from my childhood races back to my mind and I can't help but hum along . . .

"When we walk with the Lord
in the light of his Word,
what a glory he sheds on our way!
While we do his good will,
he abides with us still,
and with all who will trust and obey."[9]

My youth group experience can be bottled in 1 snapshot. It was an ordinary Wednesday night that no other person in my group probably remembers—including the 1 volunteer who helped steer the future direction of my life. Kids were entering the building getting ready for a Wednesday night service. I had shown up early, fresh from my 13th birthday party with a brand-new red Yamaha® guitar that wouldn't stay in tune for 10 seconds. I didn't know any chords, but I had shown up an hour early for worship band practice. As the adults trickled in from their day jobs and quickly started to throw a set list of songs together, it became apparent to Bill that I was not going to contribute much to the music that evening. What happened next may have been the sweetest youth ministry clinic I have ever witnessed, even though I didn't know it at the time. Bill simply showed me a C chord and said, "When I wink at you, play that guitar."

We started the program minutes later. I played the best "I Will Call Upon the Lord" that I could muster. It had lots of C chords. I was strumming and Bill was winking and God was knitting together a possibility for my life. It was a defining moment. I can't recall too many other significant steps between that night and when I joined a church staff and played guitar for 10 years as a pastor. The rest seems like a blur, but that 1 moment is forever slowed in my memory.

We never know when God is going to take a simple moment and open up a possibility for 1 kid. We obey God by investing in kids, pointing them in a direction, and walking with them for awhile. Then we trust that 1 of those teaching moments will have a profound impact on who those kids become. It is both difficult and relieving to partner with the Holy Spirit. We have to give up the control to him, but we are never alone when we speak into the lives of his children. ✦

Do This Now

1. Don't forget to stop and enjoy the sights along the road. You can quickly serve away years without ever stopping to laugh, remember, and enjoy kids. It will keep you sane and healthy as you serve.

2. Always be training someone else in your role. That doesn't mean that you are going to quit. But it is wise and good stewardship to take the things you have learned in ministry and invest in someone else. Think about who these people might be and how you can intentionally pour into them.

3. Once you feel the training you have given someone else will serve them well, don't be afraid to push them out the door. Intercede on their behalf and speak into their life about the gifts you see in them. Don't hold onto them if it's not what God has in store for them.

4. Look yourself in the mirror today and ask, "Am I doing this all for the right reasons?"

5. Have fun, disciple kids, and be God's.

Notes

1. Christian Smith, *Soul Searching: The Religious and Spiritual Lives of American Teenagers* (New York: Oxford University Press, 2005), 6, 7.
2. The Barna Update, "Small Churches Struggle to Grow Because of the People They Attract," The Barna Group Ltd., September 2, 2003, http://www.barna.org.
3. Gail A. Caissy, *Early Adolescence: Understanding the 10 to 15 Year Old* (Cambridge, MA: Perseus Publishing, 2002), 185.
4. Christian Smith, *Soul Searching: The Religious and Spiritual Lives of American Teenagers* (New York: Oxford University Press, 2005), 56, 57.
5. Ibid.
6. www.thinkexist.com Web site, "Charlie Brown quotes," http://thinkexist.com/quotes/Charlie_Brown/.
7. Norton Family Resources, "Life and Love Online—A New Report," Norton from Symantec Online, May 4, 2009, http://www.symantec.com.
8. George Barna, *Transforming Children into Spiritual Champions: Why Children Should Be Your Church's #1 Priority* (Ventura, CA: Regal, 2003), 34.
9. John H. Sammis, "Trust and Obey," 1887.

About the Author

Johnny Scott has been with Christ in Youth (CIY) for 8 years and is currently the program director of their national, jr. high-intentional touring event, Believe. He has been working with jr. high students in the local church for more than 10 years as a full-time youth pastor or volunteer. Johnny is a nationally recognized jr. high ministry leader, annually connecting with more than 2,000 youth ministers and sponsors through Believe, Christian teen conventions, and ministry training events. More importantly, Johnny works with jr. high small groups at Christ Church in Oronogo, Missouri. Johnny and his wife are the parents of 3 boys. Johnny can be reached at Johnny@ciy.com.

Christ in Youth (CIY) exists to amplify Christ's call in the lives of students to be kingdom workers. Learn more at www.ciy.com.